SPIRIT-CONTROLLED TEMPERAMENT

BY TIM LaHAYE

Tyndale
House
Publishers
Wheaton, Illinois

In Dedication

This book is dedicated to Dr. Henry Brandt, Christian psychologist of Flint, Michigan, whose biblical messages and consistent life have been used mightily of the Holy Spirit in the life of the author.

Library of Congress Card Number 67-28429
ISBN 8423-6400-5, Cloth
ISBN 8423-6401-3, Paper

Seventeenth printing, July 1974
377,000 copies in print

Printed in U.S.A.

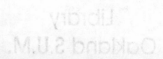

Contents

Preface

There is nothing more fascinating about man than his temperament! It is temperament that provides each human being with the distinguishing qualities of uniqueness that make him as individually different from his fellowmen as the differing designs God has given to snowflakes. It is the unseen force underlying human action, a force that can destroy a normal and productive human being unless it is disciplined and directed.

Temperament provides man with both strengths and weaknesses. Although we like to think only of our strengths, everyone has weaknesses!

God has given the Christian the Holy Spirit, who is able to improve man's natural strengths and overcome his weaknesses. The author's intent in this book, with the help of John Medina's drawings, is to help you understand how the Holy Spirit will help you overcome your weaknesses.

I am in debt to many people in the writing of this book. I have used several standard works on psychology, combined with my observations of people as pastor and counselor for 18 years, plus the speaking ministry of the Christian psychologist, Dr. Henry Brandt. I also drew extensively from a book by the Norwegian theologian, Dr. Ole Hallesby, on "Temperament and the Christian Faith."

I am grateful to numerous publishers for permission to quote from their books. Credit is given in the reference notes at the end of chapters containing the quotations.

CHAPTER 1

You're Born With It!

"Why is it that I can't control myself? I know what's right and wrong—I just don't seem to be able to do it!" This frustrated plea came from a fine young businessman who had come to me for counseling. It wasn't the first time I had heard that plaint in one form or another; in fact, it is a very common experience.

The Apostle Paul no doubt felt that same way when he said, ". . . for to will is present with me; but how to perform that which is good I find not. For the good that I would I do not: but the evil which I would not, that I do. Now if I do that I would not, it is no more I that do it, but sin that dwelleth in me." (Romans 7:18-20)

Paul differentiated between himself and that uncontrollable force within by saying, "It is no more I that do it, but sin that dwelleth in me." The "I" is Paul's person, the soul, will, and mind of man. The "sin" that dwelled in him was the natural weaknesses that he, like all human beings, inherited from his parents.

We have all inherited a basic temperament from our parents that contains both strengths and weaknesses. This temperament is called several things in the Bible, "the natural man," "the flesh," "the old man," and "corruptible flesh," to name a few. It is the basic impulse of our being that seeks to satisfy our wants. To properly understand its control of our actions and reactions we should distinguish carefully between temperament, character, and personality by defining them.

Temperament

Temperament is the combination of inborn traits that subconsciously affects man's behavior. These traits are arranged genetically on the basis of nationality, race, sex and other hereditary factors. These traits are passed on by the genes. Some psychologists suggest that we get more genes from our grandparents than our parents. That could account for the greater resemblance of some children to their grandparents than to their parents. The alignment of temperament traits is just as unpredictable as the color of eyes, hair, or size of body.

Character

Character is the real you. The Bible refers to it as "the hidden man of the heart." It is the result of your natural temperament modified by childhood training, education, and basic attitudes, beliefs, principles, and motivations. It is sometimes referred to as "the soul" of man, which is made up of the mind, emotions, and will.

Personality

Personality is the outward expression of ourselves, which may or may not be the same as our character, depending on how genuine we are. Often personality is a pleasing facade for an unpleasant or weak character. Many are acting a part today on the basis of what they think a person should be, rather than what they really are. This is a formula for mental and spiritual chaos. It is caused by following the human formula for acceptable conduct. The Bible tells us, "Man looketh on the outward appearance, and God looketh on the heart," and "Out of the heart proceed the issues of life." The place to change behavior is inside man, not outside.

In summary, temperament is the combination of traits we were born with; character is our "civilized" temperament; and personality is the "face" we show to others.

Since temperament traits are received genetically from our parents and hence are unpredictable, one should keep in mind some of the character factors that influence temperament. Nationality and race certainly play a part in one's inherited temperament. We use such expressions as, "an excitable nationality," "an industrious nationality," "a cold nationality," to describe what seems to be apparent.

While on a missionary tour to Mexico, I noticed the vast differences in the tribes that I observed. The Sapotaco Indians impressed me greatly. Many tribes had been shiftless, indifferent, and careless in their mode of life. The Sapotacos, however, were a very industrious and often ingeniously capable tribe. In one city we visited, they were actively pursuing the technical trade of weaving, and their sense of responsibility was in sharp contrast to anything we had observed in other tribesmen. The skills were learned, but the adaptability and desire to learn them were so universal throughout the tribe that it could only be an inherited trait.

A person's sex will also affect his temperament, particularly in the realm of the emotions. Women are usually considered to be more emotionally expressive than men. Even the hardest of women will weep at times, whereas some men never weep.

Temperament traits, whether controlled or uncontrolled, last throughout life. The older we get, however, the softer and more mellow our harsh and hard traits tend to become. Man learns that if he is to live at peace with his fellow man, it is best to emphasize his natural strengths and subdue his weaknesses. Many are successful in developing their character and improving their personality, but comparatively few are able to change their temperament. Yet—it is possible, as we shall see in the next chapter.

CHAPTER 2

Temperament Can Be Changed!

The Apostle Paul put into words the heart-cry of despair felt by every sincere individual who laments his weaknesses of temperament: "Oh, wretched man that I am! Who shall deliver me from the body of this death!" (Romans 7:24) His answer is electrifying, "I thank God through Jesus Christ our Lord!"

Yes, temperament can be changed! This is clearly seen from II Corinthians 5:17 where Paul wrote: "Therefore if any man be in Christ, he is a new creature: old things are passed away; behold, all things are become new."

Since temperament is our "old nature," what man needs is a "new nature." That "new nature" is imparted to man when he receives Jesus Christ into his life. The Apostle Peter could speak on this subject from personal experience, for his temperament was vastly changed by receiving the "new nature." In II Peter 1:4 he refers to those who have been "born again" by faith in Jesus Christ as having become ". . . partakers of the divine nature, having escaped the corruption that is in the world through lust." The "divine nature" which comes through Jesus Christ is the only escape from the control of our natural temperament, for only through Him are we made "new creatures."

There have been unusually self-controlled individuals who have changed part of their temperament and most of their conduct, but they have not cured all of their weaknesses. Even they have had their besetting sins. Satan knows our major temperament weaknesses, and you can be sure he will use his power to defeat us. His greatest delight in regard to Christians is to see them defeated by their own weaknesses. The victory, however, is available through Jesus Christ whose Spirit can make all things new in the believer's life.

Dr. Henry Brandt, one of the leading Christian psychologists in America, once stated to a group of ministers that if his patients would not accept Jesus Christ, he could not help them. He knew of no cure in the realm of psychology for all of man's behavior problems, but in Jesus Christ he had found the answer.

To further illustrate his absolute confidence in the power of Jesus Christ, Dr. Brandt once stated: "You can use your background as an excuse for present behavior only until you receive Jesus Christ as your personal Lord and Savior. After that you have a new power within you that is able to change your conduct."

As a pastor, I have been thrilled to see the Spirit of God take a weak, depraved temperament and transform it into a living example of the power of Jesus Christ.

Admittedly, all Christians do not experience this transforming power. Just ask a convert's husband or wife, or in some cases, children! In fact, I'm sorry to have to admit that the majority of Christians do not see a *complete* transformation of their temperament. The reason is abundantly clear: the Christian has not remained in an "abiding" relationship with Jesus Christ. (See John 15:1-14) But that does not change the fact that the moment the individual received Jesus Christ, he received the "new nature" which is able to cause "old things to pass away and all things to become new." We shall see that the filling of the Holy Spirit is not only commanded by God for every Christian (Ephesians 5:18), but this filling results in the Holy Spirit so controlling a man's nature that he actually lives the life of Christ. Before we come to that subject, however, it would be good for us to examine the basic types of temperament so we know what to expect the Holy Spirit to do with us.

CHAPTER 3

Meet The Four Basic Temperaments

More than 400 years before Christ, Hippocrates, the brilliant Greek physician and philosopher, propounded the theory that there are basically four types of temperament. He erroneously thought that these four temperament types were the result of the four body liquids that predominated in the human body: "blood"; "choler" or "yellow bile"; "melancholy" or "black bile"; and "phlegm." Hippocrates gave names to the temperaments that were suggested by the liquids he thought were the cause; the Sanguine—blood, Choleric—yellow bile, Melancholy—black bile, and Phlegmatic—phlegm. To him, these suggested the lively, active, black, and slow temperaments.

The idea that temperament is determined by body liquid has long been discarded, but strangely enough, the four-fold classification of temperaments is still widely used. Modern psychology has given many new suggestions for classification of temperaments, but none has found more acceptance than those of ancient Hippocrates. Perhaps the best known of the new classifications is the two-fold separation of "extrovert" and "introvert." These two do not provide sufficient separation for our purposes. We, therefore, shall present the four-fold temperament descriptions of Hippocrates.

The reader should bear in mind that the four-fold temperaments are basic temperaments. *No person is a single-temperament type.* We have four grandparents, all of whom make some contribution through the genes to our temperament. They may all have been of different temperaments, therefore all men are a mixture of temperaments, although usually one predominates above the rest. There are varying degrees of temperament.

For example, some may be 60 percent sanguine and 40 percent melancholy. Some are a blend of more than two, possibly all four, such as 50 percent sanguine, 30 percent choleric, 15 percent melancholy and 5 percent phlegmatic. It is impossible to determine ratios and blends, but that is not important. What is important for our purposes is to determine your basic temperament type. Then we can study your potential strengths and weaknesses, and offer a program for overcoming your weaknesses through the power of God in you.

There is a danger in presenting these four types of temperaments; some will be tempted to analyze their friends and think of them in the framework of, "What type is he?" This is a demoralizing and precarious practice. Our study of temperaments should be for *self-analysis only,* except to make us more understanding of the natural weaknesses or shortcomings of others.

Now I would like to have you turn the page and meet . . .

Sparky Sanguine

Sparky Sanguine is the warm, buoyant, lively and "enjoying" temperament. He is receptive by nature, and external impressions easily find their way to his heart, where they readily cause an outburst of response. Feelings predominate to form his decisions rather than reflective thoughts.

Mr. Sanguine has an unusual capacity to enjoy himself and usually passes on his hearty nature. When he comes into a room of people, he has a tendency to lift the spirits of everyone present by his exuberant flow of conversation. He is a thrilling story teller because his warm, emotional nature almost makes him relive the experience in the very telling of it.

Mr. Sanguine never lacks for friends. Dr. Hallesby said, "His naive, spontaneous, genial nature opens doors and hearts to him." He can genuinely feel the joys and sorrows of the person he meets and has the capacity to make him feel important, as though he were a very special friend, and he is—as is the next person he meets who then receives the same attention.

He enjoys people, does not like solitude, but is at his best surrounded by friends where he is the life of the party. He has an endless repertoire of interesting stories which he tells dramatically, making him a favorite with children as well as adults, and usually gaining him admission at the best parties or social gatherings.

Mr. Sanguine is never at a loss for words. He often speaks before thinking, but his open sincerity has a disarming effect on many of his listeners, causing them to respond to his mood. His free-wheeling, seemingly exciting, extrovertish way of life often makes him the envy of the more timid temperament types.

His noisy, blustering, friendly ways make him appear more confident than he really is, but his energy and lovable disposition gets him by the rough spots of life. People have a way of excusing his weaknesses by saying, "That's just the way Sparky is."

The world is enriched by these cheerful, sanguine people. They make good salesmen, hospital workers, teachers, conversationalists, actors, public speakers, and occasionally they are good leaders.

Now meet the second temperament type . . .

Rocky Choleric

Rocky Choleric is the hot, quick, active, practical, and strong-willed temperament. He is often self-sufficient, and very independent. He tends to be decisive and opinionated, finding it easy to make decisions for himself as well as for other people.

Mr. Choleric thrives on activity. In fact, to him, "life is activity." He does not need to be stimulated by his environment, but rather stimulates his environment with his endless ideas, plans and ambitions. His is not an aimless activity, for he has a practical, keen mind, capable of making sound, instant decisions or planning worthwhile, long-range projects. He does not vacillate under pressure of what others think. He takes a definite stand on issues and can often be found crusading against social injustice or unhealthy situations.

He is not frightened by adversities; in fact, they tend to encourage him. He has dogged determination and often succeeds where others fail, not because his plans are better than theirs, but because he is still "pushing ahead" after others have become discouraged and quit. If there is any truth in the adage, "Leaders are born, not made," then he is a born leader. Mr. Choleric's emotional nature is the least developed part of his temperament. He does not sympathize easily with others, nor does he naturally show or express compassion. He is often embarrassed or disgusted by the tears of others. He has little appreciation for the fine arts; his primary interest is in the utilitarian values of life.

He is quick to recognize opportunities and equally as quick at diagnosing the best way to make use of them. He has a well organized mind, though details usually bore him. He is not given to analysis, but rather to quick, almost intuitive appraisal; therefore, he tends to look at the goal for which he is working without seeing the potential pitfalls and obstacles in the path. Once he has started toward his goal he may run roughshod over individuals that stand in his way. He tends to be domineering and bossy and does not hesitate to use people to accomplish his ends. He is often considered an opportunist.

Mr. Choleric's attitude of self-sufficiency and strong will makes him difficult to reach for Christ in adulthood. Even after he becomes a Christian, this spirit makes it difficult for him to actively trust Christ for daily living. Choleric Christians probably find it hardest to realize what Christ meant when he said, "Without me, you can do nothing." There is no limit to what he can do when he learns to "walk in the Spirit" and to "abide in Christ."

Many of the world's great generals and leaders have been Cholerics. He makes a good executive, idea man, producer, dictator, or criminal, depending upon his moral standards.

Like Mr. Sanguine, Mr. Choleric is usually an extrovert, although somewhat less in intensity.

Now I would like to have you meet the third temperament type . . .

Maestro Melancholy

Maestro Melancholy is often referred to as the "black, or dark temperament." Actually he is the richest of all the temperaments, for he is an analytical, self-sacrificing, gifted, perfectionist type, with a very sensitive emotional nature. No one gets more enjoyment from the fine arts than the melancholy.

By nature he is prone to be an introvert, but since his feelings predominate he is given over to a variety of moods. Sometimes his moods will lift him to heights of ecstasy that cause him to act more extroverted. However, at other times he will be gloomy and depressed, and during these periods he is definitely withdrawn and can be quite antagonistic.

Mr. Melancholy is a very faithful friend, but unlike the Sanguine, he does not make friends easily. He will not push himself forward to meet people, but rather lets people come to him. He is perhaps the most dependable of all the temperaments, for his perfectionist tendencies do not permit him to be a shirker or let others down when they are depending on him. His natural reticence to put himself forward is not an indication that he doesn't like people. Like the rest of us, he not only likes others but has a strong desire to be loved by them. Disappointing experiences make him reluctant to take people at their face value, thus he is prone to be suspicious when others seek him out or shower him with attention.

His exceptional analytical ability causes him to diagnose accurately the obstacles and dangers of any project he has a part in planning. This is in sharp contrast to the Choleric, who rarely anticipates problems or difficulties, but is confident he is able to cope with whatever problems arise. This characteristic often finds the Melancholy reticent to initiate some new project or in conflict with those who wish to. Occasionally when he is in one of his great moods of emotional ecstasy or inspiration he may produce some great work of art or genius. These accomplishments are often followed by periods of great depression.

Mr. Melancholy usuallys finds his greatest meaning in life through personal sacrifice. He seems to have a desire to make himself suffer and will often choose a difficult life vocation involving great personal sacrifice. Once chosen, he is prone to be very thorough and persistent in his pursuit of it and is more than likely to accomplish great good.

No temperament has so much natural potential when energized by the Holy Spirit as the Melancholy. Many of the world's great geniuses—artists, musicians, inventors, philosophers, educators, and theoreticians, were of the melancholy temperament. It is interesting to note that many outstanding Bible characters were either predominantly melancholy in temperament or had strong melancholy tendencies, such as Moses, Elijah, Solomon, the Apostle John and many others.

Now I would have you examine the fourth temperament type . . .

Flip Phlegmatic

Flip Phlegmatic gets his name from what Hippocrates thought was the body fluid that produced that "calm, cool, slow, easy-going, well-balanced temperament." Life for him is a happy, unexcited, pleasant experience in which he avoids as much involvement as possible.

Mr. Phlegmatic is so calm and easy-going that he never seems to get ruffled, no matter what the circumstances. He has a very high boiling point and seldom explodes in anger or laughter, but keeps his emotions in control. He is the one temperament type that is consistent every time you see him. Beneath the cool, reticent, almost timid personality of Mr. Phlegmatic is a very capable combination of abilities. He feels much more emotion than appears on the surface and has a good capacity to appreciate the fine arts and the better things of life.

Mr. Phlegmatic does not lack for friends because he enjoys people and has a natural dry sense of humor. He is the type of individual that can have a crowd of people "in stitches" and never crack a smile. He has the unique capability of seeing something humorous in others and the things they do. He has a good, retentive mind and is often quite capable of being a good imitator. One of his great sources of delight is "needling" or poking fun at the other temperament types. He is annoyed by the aimless, restless enthusiasm of the Sanguine and often confronts him with his futility. He is disgusted by the gloomy moods of the Melancholy and is prone to ridicule him. He takes great delight in throwing ice water on the bubbling plans and ambitions of the Choleric.

He tends to be a spectator in life and tries not to get too involved with the activities of others. In fact, it is usually with great reluctance that he is ever motivated to any form of activity beyond his daily routine. This does not mean that he cannot appreciate the need for action and the difficulties of others. He and Mr. Choleric may see the same social injustice but their response will be entirely different. The crusading spirit of the Choleric will cause him to say, "Let's get a committee organized and campaign to do something about this!" Mr. Phlegmatic would be more likely to respond by saying, "These conditions are terrible! Why doesn't someone do something about this?" Mr. Phlegmatic is usually kindhearted and sympathetic but seldom conveys his true feelings. When once aroused to action, however, he proves to be a most capable and efficient person. He will not take leadership on his own, but when it is put on him he proves a capable leader. He has a conciliating effect on others and is a natural peace-maker.

The world has greatly benefited by the gracious nature of the efficient Phlegmatic. He makes a good diplomat, accountant, teacher, leader, scientist, or other meticulous-type worker.

Now that you have met the four temperaments, you no doubt realize why "people are individuals." Not only are there four distinct types of temperaments that produce these differences, but the combinations, mixtures and degrees of temperament multiply the possible differences. In spite of that, however, most people reveal a pattern of behavior that indicates they lean toward one basic temperament.

Recently I had an experience that graphically portrayed the difference of temperament. It was necessary for me to find a Thermofax machine while speaking at a summer high school camp. In the small town nearby, the only one available was in the Education Center. When I arrived by appointment, I found nine people hard at work. The calm, orderly and efficient surroundings made me realize that I was in the presence of individuals of a predominately Melancholy or Phlegmatic temperament.

This was later confirmed as the superintendent carefully computed my bill and refused to take my money because it was against the rules. Instead, he took me to the meticulous treasurer, who took us to the bookkeeper, who in turn relayed us to the cashier, who finally arranged for me to give my $1.44 to the switchboard operator, who kept the petty cash, lest some of their bookkeeping records would have to be altered. The clincher was the petty cash box, which clearly revealed the touch of the perfectionist. Her change had been carefully stacked in neat piles of quarters, dimes and nickels.

As I surveyed the placid environment and noted their calm but definite concern for this minor problem, my mind flitted hilariously to the scene of the sales office where they had sold the overhead projector. There the sales staff, chief executive, and all the employees were predominately of the extrovertish, Choleric or Sanguine temperaments. The place was a disorganized mess! Papers were strewn everywhere, telephones and desks unattended, the office was a hubbub of noisy activity. Finally, above the din of voices I heard the sales manager say to the staff, with a look of desperation, "One of these days we are going to get organized around here!"

These two scenes show the natural contrast of the inherited traits that produce human temperament. They also point out the fact that all four of the basic temperaments which we have described are needed to give variety and purposefulness in this world. No one temperament can be said to be better than another. *Each one contains strengths and richness, yet each one is fraught with its own weaknesses and dangers.*

Now that you have been introduced to the four temperament types, let us examine more carefully their natural strengths.

CHAPTER 4

Temperament Strengths

The Sanguine

No one enjoys life more than Sparky Sanguine! He never seems to lose his childlike curiosity for the things that surround him. Since his emotions are so receptive to his environment,

ENJOYING

even the unpleasant things of life can be forgotten by a change of environment. It is a rare ocasion when he does not awaken in a lively mood, and he will often be found whistling or singing his way through life, if his circumstances are reasonably conducive to happy thoughts. Boredom is not a part of his make-up, for he can easily turn to something that fascinates him.

The natural trait of Mr. Sanguine that produces both his hearty and optimistic disposition is defined by Dr. Hallesby: "The Sanguine person has a God-given ability to live in the

OPTIMISTIC

present." He easily forgets the past so his mind is never befogged by the memory of heartaches or disappointments. Neither is he frustrated and fearful by the apprehension of future difficulties, for he does not give the future that much thought. The Sanguine person lives for the present, consequently he is prone to be very optimistic. He has the capacity to be fascinated by little things as well as big, conse-

quently life is enjoyable today. He is always optimistic that tomorrow, whatever tomorrow holds, will be as good as today, or even better. A little thought and planning on his part today might insure that tomorrow will be even better, but that does not seem to be a part of his natural thought pattern.

He is easily inspired to engage in new plans and projects and his boundless enthusiasm often carries others along with him. If yesterday's project has failed, he is optimistic that the project he is working on today will definitely succeed.

FRIENDLY

The outgoing, handshaking, backslapping customs of the cheerful Sanguine stem basically from his genuine love for people. He enjoys being around others, sharing in their joys and sorrows, and he likes to make new friends. It distresses him to see someone who does not enjoy himself at a party and will frequently go out of his way to include this type of person in a group. His love for people is almost invariably returned.

COMPASSIONATE

One of the greatest assets of Mr. Sanguine is that he has a tender, compassionate heart. No one responds more genuinely to the needs of others than the Sanguine. He literally is able to share the emotional experiences, both good and bad, of others. He, by nature, finds it easiest to obey the Scriptural injunction, "Rejoice with those that do rejoice, and weep with those that weep." As a medical doctor, Mr. Sanguine's outstanding characteristic is his "good bedside manner."

The sincerity of Mr. Sanguine is often misunderstood by others. They are deceived by his sudden changes of emotion. They fail to understand that he is genuinely responding to the emotions of others. No one can love you more nor forget you faster than Mr. Sanguine. He has the pleasant capacity to live in the present; consequently, he enjoys life. The world is enriched by these cheerful, responsive people. When motivated and disciplined by God, they can be great servants of Jesus Christ.

The Choleric

Mr. Choleric is usually a self-disciplined individual with a strong tendency towards self-determination. He is very confident in his own ability and very aggressive. He is a man of "continual motion," but unlike the Sanguine, this activity is well planned and meaningful.

STRONG WILL POWER

Once having embarked upon a project he has a tenacious ability that keeps him doggedly driving in one direction. Of him it could rightly be said, "This one thing I do." His singleness of purpose often results in accomplishment. He may think his methods or plans are better than others but in reality his success is the result of determination, and stick-to-it-tiveness rather than superiority of planning.

The Choleric temperament is given over almost exclusively to the practical aspects of life. Everything to him is considered in the light of its utilitarian purpose and he is happiest when engaged in some worthwhile project. He has a keen mind for organization, but finds detail work distressing. He can quickly appraise a situation and diagnose the most practical solution. As a doctor, he is ideal to serve on an ambulance squad where time is at a premium in cases of emergency treatment. Many of his decisions are reached by intuition more than analytical reasoning.

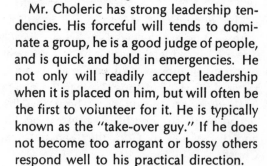

PRACTICAL

LEADER

Mr. Choleric has strong leadership tendencies. His forceful will tends to dominate a group, he is a good judge of people, and is quick and bold in emergencies. He not only will readily accept leadership when it is placed on him, but will often be the first to volunteer for it. He is typically known as the "take-over guy." If he does not become too arrogant or bossy others respond well to his practical direction.

OPTIMISTIC

Mr. Choleric's outlook on life, based on his natural feeling of self-confidence, is almost always one of optimism. He is adventuresome to the point of even leaving a secure position for the challenge of the unknown. He has a pioneering spirit.

When he appraises a situation, he does not see the pitfalls or potential problems, but merely keeps his eye on the goal. He has the unshakeable confidence that no matter what difficulties arise, he will be able to solve them. Adversity does not discourage him, instead it whets his appetite and makes him even more determined to achieve his objective.

The Melancholy

SENSITIVE

Mr. Melancholy has by far the richest and most sensitive nature of all the temperaments. He is genius-prone, that is, a higher percentage of geniuses are Melancholy than any other type. He particularly excels in the fine arts with a vast appreciation for life's true values. He is emotionally responsive but, unlike the Sanguine, is motivated to reflective thinking through his emotions.

Mr. Melancholy is particularly adept at creative thinking and at high emotional peaks will often launch into an invention or creative production that is worthwhile and wholesome.

PERFECTIONIST

Mr. Melancholy has strong perfectionist tendencies. His standard of excellence exceeds others' and his requirements of acceptability in any field are often higher than either he or anyone else can maintain. This tendency leads him to much introspection, and he often relives events and decisions made in the past, thinking how much better he would do it if given another opportunity.

ANALYTICAL

FAITHFUL FRIEND

SELF-SACRIFICING

The analytical abilities of the Melancholy, combined with his perfectionist tendencies, make him a "hound for detail." Whenever a project is suggested by a Choleric or Sanguine temperament, Mr. Melancholy can analyze it in a few moments and pick out every potential problem they will encounter. He often appears to be against things by his constant reference to potential problems. But they are real to him.

This analytical ability well qualifies him for such fields as mathematics, theoretical science, diagnostic medicine, architecture, philosophy, writing and other exacting vocations.

Those blessed with the Melancholy temperament do not have to strive to be faithful; with them it is natural. A Melancholy person usually does not attract a large number of friends as does the Sanguine, but he will keep those he attracts and would literally "lay down his life for his friends."

A Melancholy person can always be depended upon to finish his job in the prescribed time or to carry his end of the load.

Mr. Melancholy rarely seeks to be in the limelight, but prefers to do the behind-the-scenes task. He often chooses a very sacrificial vocation for life, for he has an unusual desire to give himself to the betterment of his fellow men.

Mr. Melancholy has the wonderful capacity of knowing his limitations and so rarely takes on more than he can do.

He is prone to be reserved and rarely volunteers his opinion or ideas. When asked, however, he almost always has an opinion and when it is offered, his answer indicates that he has analyzed the situation quite deeply and offers an opinion well worth hearing. He does not waste words like the Sanguine, but is usually very precise in stating exactly what he means.

The Phlegmatic

WITTY

The unexcited good humor of the Phlegmatic keeps him from being intensely involved with life and things so that he can often see humor in the most mundane experiences. His dry sense of humor evokes peals of laughter from others. He seems to have a superb inborn sense of timing in the art of humor and a stimulating imagination.

He is highly qualified by nature to be a counselor. His slow, easy-going manner makes it easy for him to listen, whereas the Sanguine and Choleric temperaments find it difficult to sit still long enough to hear the heartaches of others. He also has the ability to keep from identifying himself with the person, therefore he can be objective. He

DEPENDABLE

does not blurt out his advice, but gives thoughtful counsel well worth hearing.

Mr. Phlegmatic is dependability itself. Not only can he be depended upon to always be his cheerful, good-natured self, but he can be depended upon to fulfill his obligations and time schedules. Like the Melancholy, he is a very faithful friend and although he does not get too involved with others, he rarely proves disloyal.

PRACTICAL

Mr. Phlegmatic is also practical and efficient. He conserves his own energy by thinking, thus he early develops his capabilities to analyze a situation. Since he is not emotionally stimulated to make sudden decisions, he has a tendency to find the practical way to accomplish an obective with the least amount of effort.

He works well under pressure. In fact, he often does his best work under circumstances that would cause other temperaments to "crack."

EFFICIENT

His work always bears the hallmark of neatness and efficiency. Although he is not a perfectionist, he does have exceptionally high standards of accuracy and precision. The neatness of his desk top in the midst of a great project is always a source of amazement to the more active temperaments. But he has just found that putting everything in its exact spot is much easier and less time consuming in the long run, therefore, he is a man of orderly habits.

Summary

The variety of strengths provided by the four temperament types keeps the world functioning properly. No one temperament is more desirable than another. Each one has its vital strengths and makes its worthwhile contribution to life.

Someone facetiously pointed out this sequence of events involving the four temperaments: "The hard-driving Choleric produces the inventions of the genius-prone Melancholy, which are sold by the personable Sanguine and enjoyed by the easy-going Phlegmatic."

The strengths of the four temperaments make each of them attractive, and we can be grateful that we all possess some of these strengths. But there is more to the story! As important as are the temperament strengths, even more important, for our purposes, are their weaknesses. It is our intent in the next chapter to contrast the strengths of the temperaments with their weaknesses. Our purpose in so doing is that you diagnose your own weaknesses and develop a planned program for overcoming them.

Don't be afraid to be objective about yourself and face your weaknesses. Many people have decided what basic temperament they are at this point in the study then changed their mind when confronted with their unpleasant weaknesses. Strengths carry corresponding weaknesses, so face them realistically, then let God do something to change them.

CHAPTER 5

Weaknesses of Temperaments

The Sanguine

When studied carefully, the boundless activity of the Sanguine temperament proves to be little more than restless movement. He is often impractical and disorganized. His

RESTLESS

emotional nature can get him instantly excited and, before really analyzing the entire picture, will have him running off "half-cocked" in the wrong direction. He does not often make a good student because of this spirit of restlessness. This carries over into his spiritual life, where he finds it difficult to concentrate on reading the Word of God. His lifelong pattern of restless activity in the long run usually proves unproductive. The Sanguine person seldom lives up to his potential. Frequently his life is spent running from one tangent to another, and unless disciplined, is not lastingly productive.

WEAK-WILLED

Mr. Sanguine usually gets by on the power of his dynamic personality. But that dynamic personality is often a facade that covers a weak character. His greatest basic problem is that he is weak-willed and undisciplined. If Mr. Sanguine would discipline himself, there would be no limit to his potential in life.

He is a great one to start things and never finish them. If approached to take a Sunday School class or position in the church, his instant response is "yes." Thinking the matter through in the light of his time, abilities, and other responsibilities is not a part of his make-up. He loves to please. He does not know his limitations, and although he functions well as a "front man" for a group, without the stimulus of the group he finds it very difficult to methodically do the necessary preparatory work.

Without meaning to do so, he easily forgets his resolutions, appointments, and obligations. He cannot be depended upon to keep a time schedule or meet deadlines.

Perhaps the most dangerous result of his weak will is seen in the fact that he is prone to modify his moral principles to his surroundings and contemporaries. He is not a man of resolution or loyalty.

EGOTISTICAL

Mr. Sanguine's pleasing personality, which often makes him appear more mature in his youth than his contemporaries, gives him a prominent position early in life that can magnify his natural egotism. He can go overboard and become obnoxious by dominating, not just the major part of the conversation, but all of it. He also, through the years, has a tendency to talk more and more about himself and be occupied with things of interest to himself and think others are equally interested in them.

EMOTIONALLY UNSTABLE

The emotional instability of Mr. Sanguine can be seen in Dr. Hallesby's statement, "He is never far from tears." This is true, in spite of the fact that he is the "enjoying temperament." He discourages easily and can drift into a pattern of excusing his weaknesses or feeling sorry for himself.

His warm nature can produce spontaneous anger, and in a sudden outburst he can "fly off the handle." However, after he has exploded he will forget all about it. He is the type of person that fits the cliché often heard, "He never gets ulcers, he just gives them to everyone else." This emotional instability makes him feel genuinely sorry for his explosive outburst, and he will readily apologize. In the spiritual realm Mr. Sanguine is often found repenting for the same thing over and over again.

No one type of temperament has a greater problem with lust than does that of Mr. Sanguine. Since he is emotionally receptive, he can be tempted more easily than other types, but he is also equipped with a weak will that finds him frequently giving in to this temptation. His ability to live in the present is a danger in this regard, since he has a tendency to think more of the immediate temptation than of the wife and children at home. One of the things he should seek by the Spirit's guidance is the gift of "temperance" or "self-control." He should obey the Scriptural injunction to "flee youthful lust" and "make no provision for the flesh to fulfill the lust thereof."

Like the other three temperaments, Mr. Sanguine's greatest need is the filling of the Holy Spirit. The basic spiritual needs of the Sanguine temperament are "temperance or self-control, long-suffering, faith, peace and goodness."

The Choleric

The admirable characteristics of Mr. Choleric carry with them some serious weaknesses. The most prominent are his hard, angry, impetuous, self-sufficient traits.

Mr. Choleric has a serious emotional deficiency. Christian compassion is foreign to his nature, and he tends to be thick-skinned and unsympathetic toward other people, their dreams, accomplishments, and needs. He has a tendency to look on the sympathetic response of the Sanguine as "sentimental drivel."

HOT-TEMPERED

Much of the energy that propels the Choleric toward the attainment of his goal is generated from his hot-tempered disposition. He can become violently angry, and even after exploding his wrath upon those objects of his displeasure will continue carrying a grudge. He has been known to be very revengeful, going to almost any lengths to repay someone for an injustice done him. This angry disposition causes him much discomfort in life and can make him an undesirable person to be around. Physically he is prone to nurse an ulcer before he is forty years of age, and spiritually he grieves the Holy Spirit through bitterness, wrath and anger.

CRUEL

There is a strange streak of sheer cruelty in Mr. Choleric that causes him to run roughshod over the feelings and rights of others in his effort to achieve his purpose. Unless he is given a strong moral standard, he will not hesitate to break the law or resort to any crafty means necessary to succeed. Many of the world's most depraved criminals and dictators have been Cholerics.

Mr. Choleric's ability to be decisive also produces an impetuous tendency that causes him to get into trouble and launch programs that he is later sorry for. However, because he is so proud, he stubbornly and tenaciously sees them

IMPETUOUS

through. It is very difficult for him to apologize, and many times he will blurt out cruel, blunt, and sarcastic statements that are very cutting. It is difficult for him to show approval, and in marriage this is often one of the causes of heartache on the part of his companion. He may have so much self-control that even in his hottest fits of anger he will not strike his wife but instead use the more devastating

club of disapproval. There is nothing more devastating to a person's self-respect than being disapproved of by the person he loves most.

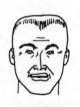

SELF-SUFFICIENT

Mr. Choleric's strong tendency toward independence and self-confidence makes him a very self-sufficient individual. A few stages of success can make him very proud, haughty, and domineering to the point where he becomes obnoxious. In spite of his capabilities, these tendencies become boring to other people and, by contrast, gives them the frustrating feeling

that they can never please him.

Unless he surrenders his life to Christ while a child, it is probably more difficult to reach a Choleric person spiritually than any other in adulthood. His spirit of self-sufficiency carries over into the spiritual realm, and he does not feel that he needs man nor God. He has a tendency to look at his accomplishments as good deeds that will more than outweigh his bad deeds performed on the way to accomplishing his goals. Even after conversion to Christ, he has a difficult time realizing that he must depend upon the Lord. When he tries to read the Bible and pray, his active mind easily leaps to planning his day's activity, and somehow, unless he is deeply impressed by the Spirit of God and sees the power of the supernatural, he looks on a regular devotional life as being somewhat impractical and a waste of his time. Of all the temperaments, he probably has the greatest number of spiritual needs, which are love, peace, gentleness, long suffering, meekness and goodness.

The Melancholy

The self-centered traits of the Melancholy temperament are superbly described by Dr. Hallesby, and for that reason I quote his entire description. "He is surely more self-centered than

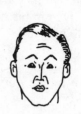

SELF-CENTERED

any of the other temperaments. He is inclined to that kind of self-examination, that kind of self-contemplation which paralyzes his will and energy. He is always dissecting himself and his own mental conditions, taking off layer after layer as an onion is peeled, until there is nothing direct and artless left in his life; there is only his everlasting self-examination. This self-examination is not only unfortunate, it is harmful. Melancholies usually drift into morbid mental conditions. They are concerned not only about their spiritual state; they are also unduly concerned about their physical condition. Everything that touches a melancholic is of prime importance to him, hence no other type can so easily become a hypochondriac."*

*Temperament and the Christian Faith. O. H. Hallesby,   1962, Augsburg, Pub. Hse.

This self-centered trait in the Melancholy, if not corrected, can actually ruin his entire life. Combined with his sensitive nature, his self-centeredness makes it very easy for him to be offended or insulted. He literally "carries his feelings on his sleeve." He is prone to be suspicious, given over to "evil surmisings." If two people are talking in hushed tones, he is almost certain to jump to the conclusion that they are talking about him. This type of thinking can lead, in severe cases, to a persecution complex.

PESSIMISTIC

Because of his perfectionist and analytical traits, Mr. Melancholy is prone to be pessimistic. He not only can see the ultimate end of a project, but what is more real to him, all of the problems that will be encountered. Many times these problems, in his mind, far outweigh the good accomplished in the whole endeavor. Not only that, he is sure that the end result will not be nearly as good as promised, and since he has been disappointed in the past, he is sure to be disappointed again.

This pessimistic outlook makes him indecisive and fearful of making decisions because he doesn't want to be wrong and fall short of his own perfectionist standards.

No one can be more critical than the Melancholy. He has the tendency to be unyielding in his expectations of other human beings and cannot happily take less than their very best. Many a perfectionist has ruined a normally good marriage because his partner measured up to only 90 percent of what was expected of her. The small part of error is looked at through his magnifying glass of perfectionism, and instead of seeing all the good, he sees an amplification of the bad. This criticism, if not spoken, is often conveyed through a proud, haughty, sometimes arrogant attitude because he looks upon people who do not share his perfectionist standards as being inferior. It should be borne in mind that he is just as critical of himself as he is of other people.

When it comes to marriage, the Melancholy often has a most difficult time making the decision to take the "fatal plunge." He is prone to "idealize" a woman from a distance, and then when he gets to know her, as lovely as she may be, he finds that she is only a human being and has her weaknesses. Many times a Melancholy will actually love the woman in spite of her weaknesses but hesitate to marry her because of them. Dr. Hallesby states, "A great many men are unmarried simply because they are Melancholic. They themselves may think that they are Melancholy because they are bachelors." The truth of the matter is they are probably bachelors because they are Melancholy.

No one manifests a greater mood change than does the Melancholy. On occasions he will be found at high emotional peaks of exuberance, but these are usually the exception and not the rule.

MOODY

More frequently, Mr. Melancholy will be found (when not energized by the Holy Spirit) to be very gloomy, depressed or going through a period of great despair. It is this common tendency that caused Hippocrates to think of him as the "black" fluid type.

This moodiness causes a vicious circle. Even those who like him when he is "acting like himself" will become annoyed or disgusted with him when, for seemingly no reason, he is going through a gloomy period. They will consequently avoid him, and his sensitive nature will immediately pick this up and plunge him into greater depths of gloom. This one trait alone can wreck the entire life of a Melancholy person unless he turns to Jesus Christ for the joy and peace that He alone can give. This moodiness is often the result of his self-centered thinking pattern, which must be changed to produce a healthy mind and make it possible for his rich and capable nature to produce its maximum potential. The gloomy moods of Mr. Melancholy often lead him into a habit of escaping present reality through the practice of day-dreaming. Because he is so dissatisfied with the imperfect present, he has a tendency to look back on the past, which becomes more pleasant the farther it gets from him. When he tires of thinking of the past, he dreams of the wonderful future. This type of thinking that lets him escape from reality is most dangerous indeed! It not only paralyzes his will and energy, but can lead to schizo-phrenia.

A Melancholy person should earnestly seek the Holy Spirit's help in getting his eyes up off himself and onto the "whitened harvest field" of needy people around him. One of the most dynamic illustrations of the power of the Gospel of the Lord Jesus Christ is to see a gloomy, moody, Melancholy person transformed by God's grace and armed with the Great Commis-sion so that he has a lofty purpose for living that directs his conscious thinking toward others rather than himself.

Another characteristic of the Melancholy temperament is that he is prone to be revengeful. In himself he finds it very difficult to forgive an affront or an insult.

REVENGEFUL

Although he appears on the surface to be calm or quiet, many times there is turbulent hatred and animosity burning within. He may never put it into action, as would a Choleric, but he may harbor this animosity and desire for revenge for many years.

This unforgiving spirit and seeking for revenge sometimes outweighs his brilliant deductive ability and causes him to make decisions on the basis of prejudice. He may seek to destroy a very worthwhile project with which he is basically in agree-ment, merely because the person leading the project has at some time in the past offended him. Although he does not generally erupt into violent anger, if animosity is harbored long enough, it may cause him to lose complete control of himself in a fit of rage.

Now that we have seen both the strengths and weaknesses of the Melancholy temperament, our attention is drawn to an interesting fact. The temperament with the greatest strengths and potential is also accompanied by what seems to be the largest of potential weaknesses. This may account for a per-sonal observation that there are very few "average" Melan-cholies. That is, a Melancholy person will utilize his strengths to the point that he stands above his fellows or he will be dominated by his weaknesses and sink beneath the level of his fellows, giving himself over to becoming a neurotic, disconsolate, or hypochondriac-type individual that neither enjoys himself nor is enjoyed by others.

Melancholy people should take great consolation in the fact that many of the most outstanding men in the Bible were predominantly Melancholy. The success, however, of all these men was that they "believed God." Faith in Christ lifts a person beyond his own temperament to the point that he lives the "new life in Christ Jesus." The primary needs of the Melancholy are love, joy, peace, goodness, faith, and self-control.

The Phlegmatic

The outstanding weakness of Mr. Phlegmatic is that he is prone to be slow and lazy. He often appears to be "dragging his feet," because he resents having been stimulated to action against his will, so he goes along just as slowly as he can.

SLOW & LAZY

His lack of motivation tends to make him a spectator in life and produces the inclination to do as little as necessary. This characteristic keeps him from initiating many of the projects that he is thinking about and very capable of executing, but to him, they just seem "too much work." The restlessness of the Sanguine and the activity of the Choleric often annoy him because he is afraid they may motivate him to work.

Because of his keen sense of humor and his ability to be a detached observer, he finds it easy to use his witty ability to tease others that annoy him or threaten to motivate him.

Dr. Hallesby has said in this regard: "If a Sanguine person enters warm and enthusiastic, the Phlegmatic person becomes cold as ice. If the Melancholic comes pessimistic and lamenting the miseries of the world, the Phlegmatic becomes more optimistic than ever and teases him beyond endurance. If a Choleric enters, brimful of his plans and projects, it is an exquisite pleasure for the Phlegmatic to throw cold water on his enthusiasm and with his

TEASE

level-headedness and keen understanding it is an easy matter for him to point out the weaknesses of the Choleric's proposition."

If he chooses he can even use his humor and wit as a decisive tool to get others all stirred up and angry while he himself never loses his composure or becomes excited.

STUBBORN

Mr. Phlegmatic often exhibits the weakness of selfishness. This trait often becomes more apparent through the years, for he learns to protect himself.

He frequently finds himself in stubborn opposition to change of any kind. His reason is that it will get him too involved. He wants to be conservative, particularly in conserving of his own energies.

As he matures, he can often learn to disguise his stubborness through his easy-going good humor, while becoming even more stubborn. Each time he is forced by the activity of others into projects and activities that turn out poorly, he becomes even more resistive to future suggestions. This stubborness has a tendency also to make him stingy and selfish, for his first thought usually is, "What is this going to cost me?" or "What will this take out of me?" Although selfishness is a basic weakness of all four temperaments, Mr. Phlegmatic is probably cursed with the heaviest dose.

INDECISIVE

Mr. Phlegmatic often becomes more indecisive through the years, caused basically by his reticence to become "involved." His practical insight and calm, analytical ability can usually find a better method for doing something, but by the time he comes up with it, one of the activists already has the group moving on their program. Therefore, he only half-heartedly enters in, in proportion to what he feels is required of him, because down in his heart he feels his plan is better.

Another thing that makes him indecisive is that even though he can analyze a situation and come to a practical method for achieving it, he will often weigh the method against whether or not he wants to get that "involved." Thus he is prone to vacillate between wanting to do something and not wanting to pay the price. This indecisive practice can soon become a deep-rooted habit that outweighs his naturally practical turn of mind.

The primary needs of the Phlegmatic are love, goodness, meekness, temperance and faith.

Summary

This completes our quick glance at the basic weaknesses of the temperaments. I hope it wasn't too discouraging. Dr. Hallesby expressed the shortcomings of the four temperaments in their relationships to other people in the following statement: "The Sanguine type enjoys people and then forgets them. The Melancholic is annoyed with people but lets them go their own crooked ways. The Choleric makes use of people for his own benefit; afterwards, he ignores them. The Phlegmatic studies people with supercilious indifference." This makes all the temperaments appear hopeless, but temperament is not character or personality or—more importantly—Spirit-controlled temperament.

Recently my wife had an experience that graphically illustrates the contrast between two of these natural temperaments. It happened while she was seated in the back of a San Diego Rapid Transit Bus. The bus stopped to pick up a passenger and was delayed an unusually long time. Several of the passengers became irritated and craned their necks to see what was holding them up. Finally, at about the point that some tempers were ready to erupt, an elderly, crippled woman came into view, paid her fare, then slowly and laboriously took her seat. When she was seated, she turned around and, with the most disarming Sanguine smile on her lovely face, said with a loud, cheery voice, "Thank you so much for waiting for me. I'm sorry I delayed you." My wife was absolutely amazed at the transformation of attitude on the part of even the most grumpy passengers as they were forced to respond with a smile to Mrs. Sanguine's cheery greeting. This dear lady had that pleasant Sanguine capacity of being able to forget the unpleasant past, not fear the unpleasant future, but to enjoy the beautiful sunshine of the present, and she made others respond to her mood.

The bus had scarcely gone two more miles when again there was a long delay. Believe it or not, another crippled woman got on the bus and took the seat directly opposite Mrs. Sanguine. My wife couldn't determine from that distance whether the second lady was a Mrs. Choleric or Mrs. Melancholy, but there was no radiance, no smile, no joy, nothing but the marks of bitterness, resentment and misery etched deeply on her face. The moment she was seated, Mrs. Sanguine got to work! Greeting her with her cheery smile, she began laughing and joking with her unhappy neighbor, and within a matter of minutes had her companion giving forth with a smile that other passengers had not believed she was capable of.

This story illustrates many things, but I would like to use it to show that circumstances do not have to determine our reactions. Our strengths or weaknesses of temperament prevail by our choice. To be sure, not all Sanguine crippled people are cheerful and not all Melancholy crippled folk are morose. But Christians can overcome natural weaknesses and enhance natural strengths through the supernatural filling of the Holy Spirit.

The Spirit-Filled Man

CHAPTER 6

The Spirit-Filled Temperament

"The fruit of the Spirit is love, joy, peace, long-suffering, gentleness, goodness, faith, meekness, temperance . . . ." Galatians 5:22-23

The Holy Spirit-filled temperament does not have weaknesses; instead it has nine all-encompassing strengths. This is man as God intends him to be. It does not matter what one's natural temperament is; any man filled with the Holy Spirit, whether Sanguine, Choleric, Melancholy or Phlegmatic, is going to manifest these nine spiritual characteristics. He will have his own natural strengths, maintaining his individuality, but he will not be dominated by his weaknesses. The nine characteristics of the Spirit will transform his weaknesses.

All of these characteristics are found illustrated in the life of Jesus Christ. He is the supreme example of the Spirit-controlled man. A fascinating study of the life of Christ would be to catalog the illustrations of these nine characteristics as they appear in the Gospels. We shall mention some as we study each characteristic.

These nine characteristics represent what God wants each one of His children to be. We shall examine each in detail that you might compare them with your present behavior. Now that you have a better and more objective look at both your strengths and weaknesses, you should be able to look to the Holy Spirit for His filling that you may become the kind of person God wants you to be. Needless to say, any individual manifesting these characteristics is going to be a happy, well-adjusted, mature and very fruitful human being. It is my conviction that there is a longing in the heart of every child of

God to live this kind of life. This life is not the result of man's effort, but the supernatural result of the Holy Spirit controlling every area of a Christian.

The first characteristic in God's catalog of Spirit-filled temperament traits is *love*. It is revealed as love both for God and for our fellowmen. The Lord Jesus said, "Thou shalt love the Lord thy God with all thy heart, and with all thy soul, and with all thy mind," and ". . . thou shalt love thy neighbor as thyself."

LOVE

Very honestly, this kind of love is supernatural! A love for God that causes a man to be more interested in the Kingdom of God than in the material kingdom in which he lives is supernatural, for man by nature is a greedy creature. Love for his fellowman, which has always been a hallmark of the devout Christian, is not limited by temperament. True, Mr. Choleric as a Christian may need to go to the Holy Spirit for love more frequently than does Mr. Sanguine, but if the Spirit controls his life, he too will be a compassionate, tenderhearted, loving individual.

There are some people with strong humanitarian tendencies by nature who have expressed love in exemplary acts. But the love described here is not just for those who stir admiration or compassion in us, but for all men. The Lord Jesus said, "Love your enemies . . . and do good to them that despitefully use you." This kind of love is never generated by man but can only be effected by God. In fact, one of the thrilling evidences of the supernatural in the Christian experience is to see two people who have "personality conflicts," which is another expression for temperament conflicts, grow to genuinely and easily love one another. The twelve apostles represented all four of the temperament types previously studied, and yet the Lord Jesus said to them, "By this shall all men know that ye are My disciples, if ye have love one for another." Many a church heartache could have been avoided had the filling of the Holy Spirit been sought for this first characteristic of the Spirit-filled temperament.

If you would like to test your love for God, try this simple method given by the Lord Jesus. He said, "If ye love Me, keep My commandments." Just ask yourself, "Am I obedient to His commandments as revealed in His Word?" If not, you are not filled with the Holy Spirit.

JOY

The second temperament characteristic of the Spirit-filled man is *joy*. R. C. H. Lenski, a great Lutheran theologian, gave this comment concerning the gracious emotion of joy. "Yes, joy is one of the cardinal Christian virtues; it deserves a place next to love. Pessimism is a grave fault. This is not fatuous joy such as the world accepts; it is the enduring joy that bubbles up from all the grace of God in our possession, from the blessedness that is ours, that is undimmed by tribulation. . . ."

The joy provided by the Holy Spirit is not limited by circumstances. Many have the mistaken idea that they can be happy if their circumstances work out properly. Really, they are confused about the difference between happiness and joy. As John Hunter of Capernwray, England, said, "Happiness is something that just happens because of the arrangement of circumstances, but joy endures in spite of circumstances."

No Christian can have joy if he depends upon the circumstances of life. The Spirit-filled life is characterized by a "looking unto Jesus, the Author and Finisher of our faith," which causes us to know that "All things work together for good to them that love God, to them that are the called according to His purpose." (Romans 8:28)

In the Scripture "joy" and "rejoicing" are frequently presented as expected forms of Christian behavior. They are not the result of self-effort but are the work of the Holy Spirit in your life, which causes you to "commit your way unto the Lord, and trust also in Him." The Psalmist said in referring to the spiritual man's experience, "Thou hast put gladness in my heart more than they have when their grain and their new wine is increased." (Psalm 4:7)

The Apostle Paul, writing from a prison dungeon, said, "Rejoice in the Lord alway: and again I say rejoice." (Philippians

4:4) The reason he could say that is because he had learned to experience the Spirit-filled life. For it was from the same prison cell the Apostle had said, "I have learned in whatsoever state I am therewith to be content." Any man that can rejoice and be content while in prison has to have a supernatural source of power! The Philippian jailer saw the genuine but supernatural joy reflected in the lives of Paul and Silas when thrown into jail for preaching the Gospel. He heard their singing and praising the Lord and must have been deeply impressed.

This "fruit" of the Spirit is woefully lacking in many Christians today, which keeps them from being fruitful in the matter of winning people to Christ, because the world must see some evidence of what Jesus Christ can do in the life of the believer today in order to be attracted to Him. This supernatural joy is available for any Christian regardless of his basic or natural temperament. Jesus said, "These things have I spoken unto you, that My joy might remain in you, and that your joy might be full." (John 15:11) He also stated in John 10:10b, "I am come that they might have life, and that they might have it more abundantly." That abundant life will reveal itself in the Christian through joy, but it is only possible as he is filled with the Holy Spirit.

Martin Luther said, "God does not like doubt and dejection. He hates dreary doctrine, gloomy and melancholy thought. God likes cheerful hearts. He did not send His Son to fill us with sadness, but to gladden our hearts. Christ says: 'Rejoice, for your names are written in heaven.'"

PEACE

The third temperament trait of the Spirit-filled man is peace. Since the Bible should always be interpreted in the light of its context, it behooves us to examine the context. The verses just preceding this in Galatians 5 describe not only the works of the natural man without the Spirit, but also his emotions. His emotional turbulence is described by ". . . hatred, variance (strivings), jealousies, wrath, divisions and envyings." We readily see that the further man gets from God, the less he knows of peace.

The "peace" spoken of here is really two-fold. Someone has described it as "peace with God" and the "peace of God." The Lord Jesus said, "Peace I leave with you, My peace I give unto you. . . ." (John 14:27) The peace He leaves us is likened to "peace with God." "My peace I give unto you" is likened to "the peace of God," for in the same verse He defines it as the peace of an untroubled heart: "Let not your heart be troubled, neither let it be afraid." The preceding verse, John 14:26, describes the coming of the Holy Spirit to believers as "the Comforter, which is the Holy Spirit." Thus we see that our Lord predicted the Holy Spirit would be the source of the "peace of God."

Peace *with* God, which is the "peace I leave with you," is the result of our salvation experience by faith. Man outside of Jesus Christ knows nothing of peace in relationship with God because his sin is ever before him and he knows he is accountable before God at the Judgment. This nagging fear robs man of peace with God all through his life. However, when this individual takes Jesus Christ at His word and invites Him into his life as Lord and Savior, Jesus Christ not only comes in as He promised to do (Revelation 3:20), but He immediately cleanses all his sin (I John 1:7,9). When the realization of God's forgiveness of his sin really grips his heart, man has peace with God. Romans 5:1 states it, "Therefore, being justified by faith, we have peace with God through our Lord Jesus Christ."

The peace *of* God, which is the antidote to worry, is not so automatically possessed by Christians as the peace *with* God. The "peace of God," which is untroubled in the face of difficult circumstances, is illustrated by the Lord Jesus who was sound asleep in the lower part of the ship while the twelve disciples were frightened beyond rationality. That ratio of twelve to one is very clearly evident among Christians today. It seems that when life's sea becomes turbulent through the raging winds of circumstance, twelve Christians will fret and fume and worry, while only one will have enough peace in his heart to trust God to take care of him in those circumstances. The twelve will be prone to worry all night, which further complicates their emotional, physical and spiritual life, while the one who "believes God" will get a good night's sleep, awaken refreshed and be available for God's use the next day. Circumstances should never produce our peace. We should look to God for peace; only He is consistent.

Just becoming a Christian does not spare us from the difficult circumstances of life. However, the Holy Spirit's presence in our lives can supply us with one of life's greatest treasures: "the peace of God," in spite of any circumstances. The Apostle Paul had this in mind when he wrote the words, "Be careful (worried or anxious) for nothing; but in everything by prayer and supplication with thanksgiving let your requests be made known unto God. And the peace of God, which passeth all understanding, shall keep your hearts and minds through Christ Jesus." (Philippians 4:6-7) An untroubled, unworried, peaceful individual facing the circumstances of life possesses a peace "which passeth all understanding." That is the "peace of God" which the Holy Spirit longs to give every believer.

These first three characteristics, *love, joy* and *peace* are emotions which very definitely counteract the most common weaknesses of temperament such as cruelty, anger, indifference, pessimism, gloom and criticism. They stand as adequate reasons for living the Spirit-filled life, but this is only the beginning.

The fourth temperament trait of the Spirit-filled man is *longsuffering*. Patience and endurance are the most prominent synonyms which have been suggested by Bible commentators for this spiritual characteristic. A very simple suggestion is, "Longsuffering means suffering long." It would be characterized by an ability to bear injuries or suffer reproof or affliction

LONGSUFFERING

without answering in kind — as the Apostle Peter said about the Lord Jesus: ". . . who, when reviled, reviles not again." This is the kind of dependability that Dr. Bob Jones must often have had in mind when using his classic statement, "The greatest ability is dependability." A longsuffering person is one who can do the menial, forgotten and difficult tasks of life without complaining or seething, but graciously, as unto the Lord. He finishes his task or suffers affronts while manifesting the loving Spirit of Christ.

The fifth characteristic of the Spirit-filled temperament is described in the King James Version as gentleness. Most of the modern translators of the Greek New Testament seem to change this to kindness or goodness, which make it almost synonymous with the next characteristic of the Spirit. In so doing, they tend to lessen the importance of this almost-forgotten form

GENTLENESS of behavior. It is a thoughtful, polite, gracious, considerate, understanding act of kindness which stems from a very tender heart. The world in which we live knows little of such tenderheartedness. It is the result of the compassion of the Holy Spirit for a lost and dying humanity.

The hurrying, bustling and pressurized life we live tends to make even some of the finest of Christians annoyed at the interruptions of "the little people." The Lord Jesus' gentle spirit serves as an illustration when contrasted with the disciples' cruel attitude toward the children who had been brought by their parents to be blessed by Him. The Scripture tells us that the disciples rebuked those who brought them, but Jesus said, "Suffer the little children to come unto Me and forbid them not." (Mark 10:13-14)

This gentle characteristic of the Holy Spirit never asks such questions as, "How often must I forgive my brother when he sins against me?" or, "Should I forgive a brother who does not ask for forgiveness?" or, "Isn't there a limit to how much a person can stand?" The Holy Spirit is able to give gentleness in the face of all kinds of pressures.

Jesus, who possessed the Holy Spirit "without measure," pictured Himself as a shepherd gently caring for easily injured sheep, and He, through His followers, tenderly cares today.

The sixth characteristic of the Spirit-filled man is called goodness, which is defined as "generous of self and possessions." It is benevolence in its purest sense. It includes hospitality and all acts of goodness that flow from the unselfish heart that is more interested in giving than receiving. Paul told Titus, the young preacher, that he should so preach that "they which have believed in God might be careful to maintain good works." (Titus 3:8) Man is so selfish by nature that he needs to be re-

minded by the Word of God and the indwelling Holy Spirit to occupy himself with goodness. It is obviously, then, a person who is more interested in doing for others than for himself.

All four of the natural temperaments are prone to be selfish and inconsiderate; thus all need this trait of goodness. It is particularly needed by those with melancholy tendencies as a cure for depression

GOODNESS

and gloom, caused by an over-indulgence in self-centered thought patterns. There is something therapeutic about doing for others that lifts a man out of the rut of self-thought. As the Lord Jesus said, "It is better to give than to receive."

Many a Christian has cheated himself out of the blessing of the Holy Spirit's inspired impulse to do something good or kind for someone else by not obeying that urge. Instead of bringing joy to someone else's life by that act of kindness, the self-centered person stifles the impulse and sinks deeper and deeper in the slough of despondency and gloom. It is one thing to get good impulses; it is quite another to transmit them into acts of goodness. D. L. Moody once stated that it was his custom, after presenting himself to the Holy Spirit and asking to be led of the Spirit, to act upon those impulses which came to his mind, provided they did not violate any known truth of Scripture. Generally speaking, that is a very good rule to follow, for it pays rich dividends in mental health in the life of the giver.

The seventh trait of the Holy Spirit-filled man is faith. It involves a complete abandonment to God and an absolute dependence upon Him. It is a perfect antidote to fear, which causes worry, anxiety and pessimism.

Some commentators suggest more than faith's being involved — namely faithfulness or dependability. But actually, a man who has Spirit-inspired faith will be faithful and dependable. The late Dr. William G. Coltman, former pastor of the Highland Park Baptist Church of Highland Park, Michigan, used to say, "When the Spirit is in control, life goes forward under the full conviction of God's ability and power."

In a vital way faith is the key to many other Christian graces. If we really believe God is able to supply all our needs, it is

52

FAITH

going to cause us to have peace and joy and will eliminate doubt, fear, striving and many other works of the flesh. Many of God's people, like the nation of Israel, waste 40 years out in the desert of life because they do not believe God. Far too many Christians have "grasshopper vision." They are like the ten faithless spies who saw the giants in the land of Canaan and came home to cry, "We are as grasshoppers in their sight." How could they possibly know what the giants thought of them? You can be sure they did not get close enough to ask! They did just what we often do — jumped to a faithless conclusion. Unbelief, which is fear, will be considered later.

The Bible teaches that there are two sources of faith. The first source is the Word of God in the life of the believer. Romans 10:17 states, "Faith cometh by hearing and hearing by the Word of God." The second is the Holy Spirit. Our text, Galatians 5:22-23, lists faith as a fruit of the Spirit. If you find that you have a temperament that is conducive to doubts, indecision and fear, then as a believer you can look to the filling of the Holy Spirit to give you a heart of faith which will dispel the emotions and actions of your natural nature, including fear, doubt, anxiety, etc. It will take time, however; habits are binding chains, but God gives us the victory in Christ Jesus. "Wait on the Lord: be of good courage, and He shall strengthen thine heart: wait, I say, on the Lord." (Psalm 27:14)

The eighth temperament trait of the Holy Spirit-filled man is meekness. The natural man is proud, haughty, arrogant, egotistical and self-centered, but when the Holy Spirit fills the life of an individual he will be humble, mild, submissive and easily entreated.

The greatest example in the world of meekness is the Lord Jesus Christ Himself. He was the Creator of the universe, and yet was willing to humble Himself, take on the form of a servant and become subject to the whims of humanity, even to the point of death, that He might purchase our redemption by His blood. Here we see the Creator of man buffeted, ridiculed, abused and spat upon by His own creation. Yet he left us an example of not reviling again.

MEEKNESS

This is particularly fortified when we recognize that all power and authority were given unto Him, even in the hours of His suffering. As He stated to Peter when He told him to put up his sword, "Thinkest thou that I cannot now pray to My Father, and He shall presently give Me more than twelve legions of angels? But how then shall the Scriptures be fulfilled, that thus it must be?" (Matthew 26:53-54) For our sakes He was meek that we might have everlasting life. He said of Himself, "I am meek and lowly in heart."

Such meekness is not natural! Only the supernatural indwelling Spirit of God could cause any of us to react to physical or emotional persecution in meekness. It is a natural tendency to assert one's self, but even the most angry temperament can be controlled by the filling of the Holy Spirit and made to manifest this admirable trait of meekness.

The final temperament trait characteristic of the Spirit-filled believer is self-control. The King James Version translates it "temperance," but really it is self-control or self-discipline. Someone has defined it as "self-controlled by the Holy Spirit."

Man's natural inclination is to follow the path of least resistance. Mr. Sanguine probably has more temptation along this line than any of the other temperament types, though who of us can say he has not given in to this very common temptation? "Self-control" will solve the Christian's problem of emotional outbursts such as rage, anger, fear, jealousy, etc., and cause him to avoid emotional excesses of any kind. The Spirit-controlled temperament will be one that is consistent, dependable and well ordered.

It has occurred to me that all four of the basic temperament types have a common difficulty that will be overcome by the Spirit-filled trait of self-control. That weakness is an inconsistent or ineffective devotional life. No Christian can be mature in Christ, steadily filled with the Holy Spirit and usable in the hand of God, who does not regularly feed on the Word of God. Evangelical Christians would overwhelmingly confirm this fact, even though a very small percentage of Christians have a quiet time with any degree of regularity.

Mr. Sanguine is too restless and weak-willed by nature to be consistent in anything, much less in getting up a few minutes early to have a regular time of Bible reading and prayer.

Mr. Choleric has the strong will power to be consistent in anything he sets his mind to, but his problem is in seeing the need for such a practice. He is by nature

SELF-CONTROL

such a self-confident individual that even after he is converted it takes some time for him to realize personally what the Lord Jesus meant when He said, "Without Me, ye can do nothing." Even when he sees the need and begins to have a regular devotional life, he has to fight the temptation to keep his practical, active mind from flitting off into many other directions or planning his day's activities when he is supposed to be reading the Word, praying or listening to the Sunday sermon.

Mr. Melancholy is perhaps most likely of the four to be regular in his devotional life, except that his analytical ability often sends him off in the quest of some abstract, theologically hairsplitting truth rather than letting God speak to him concerning his personal needs from the mirror of His truth. His regular prayer life can become a time of complaining and mourning to God about what he considers his unhappy state of affairs as he nurses his grudges and reviews his difficulties. Thus his devotional life can conceivably thrust him into greater periods of despair than he was in before. However, when controlled by the Holy Spirit, his prayer life will be characterized by "giving thanks" (I Thessalonians 5:18) and compliance with "Rejoice in the Lord always, and again I say rejoice." (Philippians 4:4)

Mr. Phlegmatic is prone to recommend a regular quiet time as a necessary part of the Christian life, but if his slow, indolent and often indifferent inclination is not disciplined by the Holy Spirit, he will never quite get around to a regular feeding on God's Word.

As you look at these nine admirable traits of the Spirit-filled man, you not only get a picture of what God wants you to be, but what He is willing to make you in spite of your natural temperament. It should, however, be borne in mind that no amount of self-improvement or self-effort can bring any of these traits into our lives without the power of the Holy Spirit. From this we conclude that the most important single thing in the life of any Christian is to be filled with the Holy Spirit. The supreme question, then, comes to mind: How can I be filled with the Holy Spirit? The answer to that question will be seen in our next chapter.

CHAPTER 7

How To Be Filled With The Holy Spirit

The most important thing in the life of any Christian is to be filled with the Holy Spirit! The Lord Jesus said, "Without Me ye can do nothing." Christ is in believers in the person of His Holy Spirit. Therefore, if we are filled with His Spirit, He works fruitfully through us. If we are not filled with the Holy Spirit, we are unproductive.

It is almost impossible to exaggerate how dependent we are on the Holy Spirit. We are dependent on Him for convicting us of sin before and after our salvation, for giving us understanding of the Gospel, causing us to be born again, empowering us to witness, guiding us in our prayer life—in fact, for everything. It is no wonder that evil spirits have tried to counterfeit the work of the Holy Spirit and confuse His work.

There is probably no subject in the Bible upon which there is more confusion today than that of being filled with the Holy Spirit. There are many fine Christian people who seem to equate the filling of the Holy Spirit with speaking in tongues or some emotionally ecstatic experience. There are other Christians who because of excesses observed or heard of in this direction have all but eliminated the teaching of the filling of the Holy Spirit. They just do not recognize His importance in their lives.

Satan places two obstacles before men: (1) he tries to keep them from receiving Christ as Savior, and (2) if he fails in this, he then tries to keep men from understanding the importance and work of the Holy Spirit. Once a man is converted, Satan seems to have two different approaches. He tries to get men to associate the filling of the Holy Spirit with emotional excesses, or, the opposite swing of the pendulum, to ignore the Holy Spirit altogether.

One of the false impressions gained from people and not from the Word of God is that there is some special "feeling" when one is filled with the Holy Spirit. Before we examine how to be filled with the Holy Spirit, let us find what the Bible teaches we can expect when we are filled with the Holy Spirit.

What To Expect When Filled With The Holy Spirit

1. The nine temperament traits of the Spirit-filled life. (Galatians 5:22-23)

We have already examined these traits in detail in Chapter 6, but their presence in the believer's life bears further emphasis. Any individual who is filled with the Holy Spirit is going to manifest these characteristics! He does not have to try to, or play a part, or act out a role; he will just be this way when the Spirit has control of his nature.

Many who claim to have had the "filling," or as some call it, "the anointing," know nothing of love, joy, peace, longsuffering, gentleness, goodness, meekness, faith, or self-control. These are, however, the hallmark of the person filled with the Holy Spirit!

2. A joyful, thanks-giving heart and a submissive spirit. (Ephesians 5:18-21)

When the Holy Spirit fills the life of a believer, the Bible tells us He will cause him to have a singing, thanks-giving heart and a submissive spirit.

> "And be not drunk with wine, wherein is excess; but be filled with the Spirit;
> "Speaking to yourselves in psalms and hymns and spiritual songs, singing and making melody in your heart to the Lord;
> "Giving thanks always for all things unto God and the Father in the name of our Lord, Jesus Christ;
> "Submitting yourselves one to another in the fear of God."

A singing, thanks-giving heart and a submissive spirit, independent of circumstances, are so unnatural that they can only be ours through the filling of the Holy Spirit. The Spirit of God is able to change the gloomy or griping heart into a song-filled, thankful heart. He is also able to solve man's natural rebellion problem by increasing his faith to the point that he really believes the best way to live is in submission to the will of God.

The same three results of the Spirit-filled life are also the results of the Word-filled life, as found in Colossians 3:16-18.

> "Let the word of Christ dwell in you richly in all wisdom; teaching and admonishing one another in psalms and hymns and spiritual songs, singing with grace in your hearts to the Lord.
> "And whatsoever ye do in word or deed, do all in the name of the Lord Jesus, giving thanks to God and the Father by Him.
> "Wives, submit yourselves unto your own husbands, as it is fit in the Lord."

It is no accident that we find the results of the Spirit-filled life (Ephesians 5:18-21) and those of the Word-filled life to be one and the same. The Lord Jesus said that the Holy Spirit is "the Spirit of Truth," and He also said of the Word of God, "Thy Word is Truth." It is easily understood why the Word-filled life causes the same results as the Spirit-filled life, for the Holy Spirit is the author of the Word of God. This highlights the error of those who try to receive the Holy Spirit through a once-for-all experience rather than an intimate relationship with God which Jesus described as "abiding in Me." This relationship is possible in the Christian's life as God communes with him and fills his life through the "Word of Truth" and he communes with God in prayer guided by the "Spirit of Truth." The conclusion that we can clearly draw here is that the Christian who is Spirit-filled will be Word-filled, and the Word-filled Christian who obeys the Spirit will be Spirit-filled.

3. The Holy Spirit gives us power to witness. (Acts 1:8)

> "But ye shall receive power, after that the Holy Ghost is come upon you: and ye shall be witnesses unto Me both in Jerusalem, and in all Judaea, and in Samaria, and unto the uttermost part of the earth."

The Lord Jesus told His disciples that "It is expedient (necessary) for you that I go away; for if I go not away, the Comforter (Holy Spirit) will not come unto you." (John 16:7) That explains why the last thing Jesus did before He ascended into heaven was to tell His disciples, "But ye shall receive power, after that the Holy Spirit is come upon you: and ye shall be witnesses unto Me . . . ."

Even though the disciples had spent three years with Jesus personally, had heard His messages several times, and were the best trained witnesses He had, He still instructed them "not to depart from Jerusalem, but wait for the promise of the Father." (Acts 1:4) All of their training obviously was incapable of producing fruit of itself without the power of the Holy Spirit. It is well known that when the Holy Spirit came on the day of Pentecost, they witnessed in His power, and three thousand persons were saved.

We too can expect to have power to witness when filled with the Holy Spirit. Would to God that there was as much desire on the part of God's people to be empowered to witness in the Spirit as there is to have some ecstatic or emotional experience with the Holy Spirit.

The power to witness in the Holy Spirit is not always discernable, but must be accepted by faith. When we have met the conditions for the filling of the Holy Spirit, we should be careful to believe we have witnessed in the power of the Spirit whether or not we see the results. Because the Holy Spirit demonstrated His presence on the day of Pentecost so dramatically and because occasionally we see the evidence of the Holy Spirit in our lives, we come to think that it should always be obvious, but that is not true. It is possible to witness in the power of the Holy Spirit and still not see an individual come to a saving knowledge of Christ. For in the sovereign plan of God He has chosen never to violate the right of man's free choice. Therefore, a man can be witnessed to in the power of the Holy Spirit and still reject the Savior. The witness may then go away with the erroneous idea of having been powerless merely because he was unsuccessful. We cannot always equate success in witnessing with the power to witness!

Recently it was my privilege to witness to an 80-year-old man. Because of his age and a particular problem, I made a special effort to meet the conditions of being filled with the Holy Spirit before I went to his home. He paid very close attention as I presented the Gospel by using the "four spiritual laws." When I finished and asked if he would like to receive Christ right then, he said, "No, I'm not ready yet." I went away amazed that a man 80 years of age could say he was "not ready yet" and concluded that I did not witness in the power of the Holy Spirit.

A short time later I went back to see the man and found that he had passed his 81st birthday. Once again I started to present the Gospel to him, but he informed me that he had received Christ. He had restudied the four spiritual laws which I had written out on a sheet of paper, and alone in his room he got down on his knees and invited Christ Jesus into his life as Savior and Lord. Afterward, I wondered how many other times in my life, because I had not seen an immediate response to the Gospel, I had wrongly concluded that the Spirit had not filled me with His power to witness.

To be sure, a Christian life, when filled with the Holy Spirit, will produce fruit. For if you examine what Jesus referred to as "abide in Me" (John 15) and what the Bible teaches in relationship to being "filled with the Spirit," you will find they are one and the same experience. Jesus said, "He that abideth in Me and I in him, the same bringeth forth much fruit . . . ." Therefore, we can conclude that the abiding life or the Spirit-filled life will produce fruit. But it is wrong to require every witnessing opportunity to demonstrate whether or not we are empowered by the Spirit to witness. Instead, we must meet the conditions for the filling of the Holy Spirit and then believe, not by results or sight or feeling, but by faith, that we are filled.

4. The Holy Spirit will glorify Jesus Christ. (John 16:13-14)

> "Howbeit when He, the Spirit of truth, is come, He will guide you into all truth; for He shall not speak of Himself; but whatsoever He shall hear, that shall He speak: and He will shew you things to come.
>
> "He shall glorify Me: for He shall receive of Mine, and shall shew it unto you."

A fundamental principle should always be kept in mind regarding the work of the Holy Spirit: He does not glorify Himself, but the Lord Jesus Christ. Any time anyone but the

Lord Jesus receives the glory, you can be sure that what is done is not done in the power of or under the direction of the Holy Spirit, for His express work is to glorify Jesus. This test should always be given to any work that claims to be the work of God's Holy Spirit.

The late F. B. Meyer told the story of a woman missionary who came to him at a Bible conference after he had spoken on the subject of how to be filled with the Holy Spirit. She confessed that she was never consciously filled with the Holy Spirit and was going to go up to the prayer chapel and spend the day in soul-searching to see if she could receive His filling.

Late that evening she came back just as Meyer was leaving the auditorium. He asked "How was it, sister?" and she said, "I'm not quite sure." He then asked what she did, and she explained her day's activities of reading the Word, praying, confessing her sins and asking for the filling of the Holy Spirit. She then stated, "I do not feel filled with the Holy Spirit." Meyer asked her, "Tell me, sister, how is it between you and the Lord Jesus?" Her face lit up and with a smile she said, "Oh, Dr. Meyer, I have never had a more blessed time of fellowship with the Lord Jesus in all of my life." To which he replied, "Sister, that is the Holy Spirit!" The Holy Spirit will always make the believer more conscious of the Lord Jesus than Himself.

Now, in review, let us summarize what we can expect when filled with the Holy Spirit. Very simply, it is the nine temperament characteristics of the Spirit, a singing, thanks-giving heart that gives us a submissive attitude, and the power to witness. These characteristics will glorify the Lord Jesus Christ. What about "feeling" or "ecstatic experiences"? The Bible does not tell us to expect these things when we are filled with the Holy Spirit; therefore, we should not expect that which the Bible does not promise.

How To Be Filled With The Holy Spirit

The filling of the Holy Spirit is not optional equipment in the Christian life, but a command of God! Ephesians 5:18 tells us, "And be not drunk with wine, wherein is excess, but be filled with the Spirit." This statement is in the imperative mood; thus we should accept it as a command.

God never makes it impossible for us to keep His commandments. So, obviously, if He commands us to be filled with the Holy Spirit, and He does, then it must be possible for us to be filled with His Spirit. I would like to give five simple steps for being filled with the Holy Spirit:

1. Self-examination (Acts 20:28 and I Corinthians 11:28)

The Christian interested in the filling of the Holy Spirit must regularly "take heed" to "examine himself." He should examine himself, not to see if he measures up to the standards of other people or the traditions and requirements of his church, but to the previously mentioned results of being filled with the Holy Spirit. If he does not find he is glorifying Jesus, if he does not have power to witness, or if he lacks a joyful, submissive spirit or the nine temperament traits of the Holy Spirit, then his self-examination will reveal those areas in which he is deficient and will uncover the sin that causes them.

2. Confession of all known sin (I John 1:9)

"If we confess our sins, He is faithful and just to forgive us our sins, and to cleanse us from all unrighteousness."

The Bible does not put an evaluation on one sin or another, but seems to judge all sin alike. After examining ourselves in the light of the Word of God, we should confess all sin brought to mind by the Holy Spirit, including those characteristics of the Spirit-filled life that we lack. Until we start calling our lack of compassion, our lack of self-control, our lack of humility, our anger instead of gentleness, our bitterness instead of kindness, and our unbelief instead of faith, as sin, we will never have the filling of the Holy Spirit. However, the moment we recognize these deficiencies as sin and confess them to God, He will "cleanse us from all unrighteousness." Until we have done this we cannot have the filling of the Holy Spirit, for He fills only clean vessels. (II Timothy 2:21)

3. Submit yourself completely to God (Romans 6:11-13)

"Likewise reckon ye also yourselves to be dead indeed unto sin, but alive unto God through Jesus Christ our Lord.

"Let not sin therefore reign in your mortal body, that ye should obey it in the lusts thereof.

"Neither yield ye your members as instruments of unrighteousness unto sin: but yield yourselves unto God, as those that are alive from the dead, and your members as instruments of righteousness unto God."

To be filled with the Holy Spirit, one must make himself completely available to God to do anything the Holy Spirit directs him to do. If there is anything in your life that you are unwilling to do or to be, then you are resisting God, and this always limits God's Spirit! Do not make the mistake of being afraid to give yourself to God! Romans 8:32 tells us, "He that spared not His own Son, but delivered Him up for us all, how shall He not with Him also freely give us all things?" It is clear from this verse that if God loved us so much as to give His Son to die for us, certainly He is interested in nothing but our good; therefore, we can trust Him with our lives. You will never find a miserable Christian in the center of the will of God, for He will always accompany His directions with an appetite and desire to do His will.

Resisting the Lord through rebellion obviously stifles the filling of the Spirit. Israel limited the Lord, not only through unbelief, but, as Psalm 78:8 tells us, by becoming a "stubborn and rebellious generation; a generation that set not their heart aright and whose spirit was not steadfast with God." All resistance to the will of God will keep us from being filled with the Holy Spirit. To be filled with His Spirit, we must yield ourselves to His Spirit just as a man yields himself to wine for its filling.

Ephesians 5:18 says, "Be not drunk with wine . . . but be filled with the Spirit." When a man is drunk, he is dominated by alcohol; he lives and acts, and is dominated by its influence. So with the filling of the Holy Spirit, man's actions must be dominated by and dictated by the Holy Spirit. For consecrated Christians this is often the most difficult thing to do, for we can always find some worthy purpose for our lives, not realizing that we are often filled with ourselves rather than with the Holy Spirit, as we seek to serve the Lord.

This summer, while speaking at a high school and college camp, we had a thrilling testimony from a ministerial student who said that for the first time he realized what it meant to be filled with the Holy Spirit. As far as he knew, he had not been guilty of the usual sins of the carnal Christian. Actually, he had only one area of resistance in his life. He loved to preach, and the possibilities of being a pastor or evangelist appealed to him very much, but he did not want the Lord to make a missionary out of him. During that week the Holy Spirit spoke to the lad about that very vocation, and when he submitted everything to the Lord and said, "Yes, I'll go to the ends of the earth," for the first time he experienced the true filling of the Holy Spirit. He then went on to say, "I don't believe the Lord wants me to be a missionary after all; He just wanted me to be willing to be a missionary."

When you give your life to God, do not attach any strings or conditions to it. He is such a God of love that you can safely give yourself without reservation, knowing that His plan and use of your life is far better than yours. And, remember, the attitude of yieldedness is absolutely necessary for the filling of God's Spirit. Your will is the will of the flesh, and the Bible says that "the flesh profiteth nothing."

Yieldedness is sometimes difficult to determine when once we have solved the five big questions of life: (1) Where shall I attend college? (2) What vocation shall I pursue? (3) Whom shall I marry? (4) Where shall I live? (5) Where shall I attend church? A Spirit-filled Christian will be sensitive to the Spirit's leading in small decisions as well as the big ones. But it has been my observation that many Christians who have made the right decisions on life's five big questions are still not filled with the Spirit.

Someone has suggested that being yielded to the Spirit is being available to the Spirit. Peter and John in Acts 3 make a good example of that. They were on their way to the temple to pray when they saw the lame man begging alms. Because they were sensitive to the Holy Spirit, they healed him "in the name of Jesus Christ of Nazareth." The man began leaping about and praising God until a crowd gathered. Peter, still sensitive to the Holy Spirit, began preaching; "many of them which heard the Word believed; and the number of the men was about five thousand." (Acts 4:4)

Many times I fear we are so engrossed in some good Christian activity that we are not "available" when the Spirit leads. In my own life, I have found that when someone asks me to do some good thing and I give a negative response, it is the flesh rather than the Spirit. Many a Christian has said "no" to the Holy Spirit when He offered an opportunity to teach Sunday School. It may have been the Sunday school superintendent that asked, but he too had been seeking the leading of the Holy Spirit. Many a Christian says, "Lord, here am I, use me!" but when asked to go calling or witnessing is too busy painting, bowling or pursuing some other activity that interferes. What is the problem? He just isn't available. When a Christian yields himself unto God, "as those that are alive from the dead," he takes time to do what the Spirit directs him to do.

4. Ask to be filled with the Holy Spirit (Luke 11:13)

> *"If ye, then, being evil, know how to give good gifts unto your children: how much more shall your heavenly Father give the Holy Spirit to them that ask Him?"*

When a Christian has examined himself, confessed all known sin and yielded himself without reservation to God, he is then ready to do the one thing he must do to receive the Spirit of God. Very simply, it is to ask to be filled with the Spirit. Any suggestion to present-day believers of waiting or tarrying or laboring or suffering is man's suggestion. Only the disciples were told to wait, and that was because the day of Pentecost had not yet come. Since that day, God's children have only to ask for His filling to experience it.

The Lord Jesus compares this to our treatment of our earthly children. Certainly a good father would not make his children beg for something he commanded them to have. How much less does God make us beg to be filled with the Holy Spirit which He has commanded. It is just as simple as that! But don't forget Step 5.

5. Believe you are filled with the Holy Spirit! And thank Him for His filling.

> *"And he that doubteth is damned if he eat, because he eateth not of faith: for whatsoever is not of faith is sin." (Romans 14:23)*
> *"In everything give thanks: for this is the will of God in Christ Jesus concerning you." (I Thessalonians 5:18)*

For many Christians the battle is won or lost right here. After examining themselves, confessing all known sin, yielding themselves to God and asking for His filling, they are faced with a decision: to believe they are filled, or to go away in unbelief, in which case they have sinned, for "whatsoever is not of faith is sin."

The same Christian, who when doing personal work tells the new convert to "take God at His Word concerning salvation," finds it difficult to heed his own advice concerning the filling of the Holy Spirit. He will tell a new babe in Christ, who lacks assurance of salvation, that he can know that Christ is in his life because He promised to come in if He were invited, and "God always keeps His Word." Oh, that the same sincere personal worker would believe God when He says: "How much more shall your heavenly Father give the Holy Spirit to them that ask Him?" If you have fulfilled the first four steps, then thank God for His filling by faith. Don't wait for feelings, don't wait for any physical signs, but fasten your faith to the Word of God that is independent of feeling. Feelings of assurance of the Spirit's filling often follow our taking God at His Word and believing He has filled us, but they neither cause the filling nor determine whether or not we are filled. Believing we are filled with the Spirit is merely taking God at His Word, and that is the only absolute this world has. (Matthew 24:35)

Walking in The Spirit

> "This I say then, Walk in the Spirit, and ye shall not fulfill the lust of the flesh." (Galatians 5:16)
> "If we live in the Spirit, let us also walk in the Spirit." (Galatians 5:25)

"Walking in the Spirit" and being filled by the Holy Spirit are not one and the same thing, though they are very closely related. Having followed the five simple rules for the filling of the Holy Spirit, one may walk in the Spirit by guarding against quenching or grieving the Spirit (as we will describe in the next two chapters) and by following the above five steps each time he is aware that sin has crept into his life. Being filled with the Holy Spirit is not a single experience that lasts for life. On the contrary, it must be repeated many times. In fact, at first it should be repeated many times daily. This can be done while kneeling at your place of devotion, at the breakfast table, in the car en route to work, while sweeping the kitchen floor, while listening to a telephone conversation—in fact, anywhere. In effect, walking in the Spirit puts one in continual communion with God, which is the same as abiding in Christ. To "walk in the Spirit" is to be freed of your weaknesses. Yes, even your greatest weaknesses can be overcome by the Holy Spirit (Chapter 10). Instead of being dominated by your weaknesses, you can be dominated by the Holy Spirit. That is God's will for all believers!

CHAPTER 8

Grieving The Holy Spirit Through Anger

> *"Let no corrupt communication proceed out of your mouth, but that which is good to the use of edifying, that it may minister grace unto the hearers.*
> *"And grieve not the holy Spirit of God, whereby ye are sealed unto the day of redemption.*
> *"Let all bitterness, and wrath, and anger, and clamor, and evil speaking, be put away from you, with all malice:*
> *"And be ye kind one to another, tenderhearted, forgiving one another, even as God for Christ's sake hath forgiven you." (Ephesians 4:29-32)*

Grieving the Holy Spirit through anger, bitterness, wrath or other forms of human cussedness probably ruins more Christian testimonies than any other kind of sin.

This text makes it very clear that we "grieve" the Holy Spirit of God through bitterness, wrath, anger, clamor, evil speaking and malice, which is enmity of heart. For some reason, otherwise consecrated Christians seem reluctant to face as sin these emotions that stem from anger. Instead, it is common to stop advancement in the Christian life with victory over such external habits as drinking, gambling, profanity, etc., without coming to grips with the emotions that churn within. Although unseen, anger is every bit as much a sin as these overt practices. Galatians 5:20 lists hatred, strife and wrath in the same category as murders, drunkenness and revellings, saying, ". . .of the which I tell you before as I have also told you in time past, that they which do such things shall not inherit the Kingdom of God."

Anger—A Universal Sin

Anger is one of two universal sins of mankind. After counseling several hundred people, I have concluded that all emotional tension can be traced to one of two things: anger or fear. I cannot think of a single case involving individuals or couples who were upset but that the basic problem stemmed from an attitude that was angry, bitter and vitriolic, or fearful, anxious, worried and depressed. I have dealt with some people who were both angry and fearful. Dr. Henry Brandt, in his book *The Struggle for Peace,* points out that anger can cause a person to become fearful. Dr. Raymond L. Cramer, another Christian psychologist, says in his book *The Psychology of Jesus and Mental Health:* "At times anxiety expresses itself in anger. A tense, anxious person is much more likely to become irritable and angry."[1] Anxiety is a form of fear; therefore, from these two Christian psychologists we can conclude that an angry person can also become a fearful person, and a fearful person can become an angry person. Anger grieves the Holy Spirit, and fear quenches the Holy Spirit, as we will point out in the next chapter.

In our study of the temperaments we found that the extrovertish sanguine and choleric temperaments are angry-prone, while the melancholy and phlegmatic are fear-prone. Since most people are a combination of temperaments, they could well have a natural predisposition to both fear and anger—if, for example, they are predominantly sanguine with possibly 30 percent melancholy tendencies. Then, too, from the statements cited from Dr. Brandt and Dr. Cramer, it would seem that the angry-prone temperament's expression of anger could cause fear, and the indulgence of the fear-prone habit of the melancholy and phlegmatic temperaments could cause the emotional problems of anger and hostility. It is my personal opinion that these two emotions bring more Christians into bondage to the law of sin than any other emotions or desires.

Thank God there is a cure for these weaknesses through the Holy Spirit!

The High Cost of Anger

If man really understood the high price paid for pent-up wrath or bitterness and anger, he would seek some remedy for it. We shall consider the high cost of anger emotionally, socially, physically, financially, and most important of all, spiritually.

A. Emotionally

Suppressed anger and bitterness can make a person emotionally upset until he is "not himself." In this state he often makes decisions that are harmful, wasteful or embarrassing. We are intensely emotional creatures, designed so by God, but if we permit anger to dominate us, it will squelch the richer emotion of love. Many a man takes his office grudges and irritations home and unconsciously lets this anger curtail what could be a free-flowing expression of love for his wife and children. Instead of enjoying his family and being enjoyed by them, he allows his mind and emotions to mull over the vexations of the day. Life is too short and our moments at home too brief to pay such a price for anger.

Dr. S. I. McMillen, a Christian medical doctor, has written a very interesting book entitled *None of These Diseases*. There he makes these interesting statements:

"The moment I start hating a man, I become his slave. I can't enjoy my work any more because he even controls my thoughts. My resentments produce too many stress hormones in my body and I become fatigued after only a few hours' work. The work I formerly enjoyed is now drudgery. Even vacations cease to give me pleasure . . . the man I hate hounds me wherever I go. I can't escape his tyrannical grasp on my mind. When the waiter serves me porterhouse steak with french fries, asparagus, crisp salad, and strawberry shortcake smothered with ice cream, it might as well be stale bread and water. My teeth chew the food and I swallow it, but the man I hate will not permit me to enjoy it . . . the man I hate may be many miles from my bedroom, but more cruel than any slavedriver, he whips my thoughts into such a frenzy that my innerspring mattress becomes a rack of torture."[2]

Anger takes many forms. Many people do not regard themselves as angry individuals because they don't understand the many disguises anger takes. Consult the following chart for a description of the 16 variations of anger.

Bitterness	Wrath
Malice	Hatred
Clamor	Seditions
Envy	Jealousy
Resentment	Attack
Intolerance	Gossip
Criticism	Sarcasm
Revenge	Unforgiveness

B. Socially

Very simply, an angry person is not pleasant to be around; consequently, those who are angry, grumpy or disgruntled are gradually weeded out of the social lists or excluded from the fun times of life. This is a price that a partner is often asked to pay for the anger of his mate, which in turn may increase their anger toward each other and limit what otherwise could be an enjoyable relationship.

The social price paid for inner anger and bitterness is seen more clearly in detail as a person progresses in age. We have often heard someone ask the question, "Have you noticed how ornery and cranky Granddad is getting in his old age?" What seems to be a change is not a change at all. Granddad just loses some of his inhibitions and the desire to please others as he grows older and reverts more to the candid reactions of childhood. Children do not try to hide their feelings, but express them, and elderly people return again to this same custom. Granddad begins to act the way he has felt all his life. This bitter, resentful and often self-pitying spirit makes him unbearable to have around, which in turn makes life more difficult for him in his old age. What a tragedy if Granddad is a Christian and did not let God's Holy Spirit "mortify the deeds of the flesh" many years before.

C. Physically

It is difficult to separate the physical price paid for anger from the financial, because anger and bitterness produce so much stress which in turn causes physical disorder so that thousands of dollars are spent needlessly by Christian people for doctors and drugs. Doctors and medical associations today have released various statistics showing that from 60 to as high as 90 percent of man's bodily illness is emotionally induced, and anger and fear are the main culprits! (Just think of the missionaries that could be sent to the foreign fields and the churches that could be built with 60 percent of the money Christians pay for medical expenses.)

If doctors are correct in their estimates, and we have no reason to believe they are not, this is money and talent wasted. How can our emotions actually cause physical illness? Very simply, for our entire physical body is intricately tied up with our nervous system. Whenever the nervous system becomes tense through anger or fear, it adversely affects one or more parts of the body. Both Dr. McMillen and Dr. Brandt refer in their books to an illustrated example drawn by Dr. O. Spurgeon English in his book *The Automatic Nervous System*. The following example based upon the works of the flesh described in Galatians 5 and Ephesians 4 was inspired somewhat by Dr. English's illustration.

Proverbs 4:23 says, "Keep thy heart with all diligence; for out of it are the issues of life." Therefore, the heart to which the writer of Proverbs referred was not the blood-pumping station we recognize as keeping our body in motion, but the emotional center located between our temples. In order for any body movement to take place, a message must be conveyed from the emotional center to the member to be moved. This message is given with lightning-like speed, and we are not conscious of the source from which it originates. For example, when a shortstop sees the flash of a ball to his left, his body, arms and legs seem to move in one coordinated movement spontaneously, but it has not been spontaneous at all; before he ever moved a muscle, his emotional center sent its impulses of action through the nervous system, notifying his members precisely what to do in that given situation.

If the emotional center is normal, then the functions of the body will be normal. If, however, the emotional center is "upset" or behaves in an abnormal manner, a reaction will be generated through the nervous system to almost every part of the body.

A Man Without Christ

This drawing of a man without Christ shows the three most important parts of man's being: the will, the mind and the heart (or emotional center). Man is affected emotionally by what is placed in his mind. What he places in his mind is determined by his will; therefore, if man wills to disobey God and records things on the files of his mind that cause emotions contrary to the will of God, these emotions trigger actions that displease God.

All sin begins in the mind! Man never commits sin spontaneously. Long before man commits murder he has harbored hatred, anger and bitterness in his mind. Before he commits adultery he has harbored lust in his mind. Filthy pornographic literature stimulates the mind to evil, whereas the Word of God calms the emotions of man and leads him in the ways of righteousness. Someone has said, "You are what you read." Man chooses through his will whether to read pornographic literature or something wholesome such as the Bible. His mind receives whatever his will chooses to read or hear, and his emotions will be affected by whatever he puts in his mind. That is why Jesus Christ gave the challenge to man, "Thou shalt love the Lord thy God with all thy heart, with all thy soul (will) and with all thy mind."

A Man Without Christ

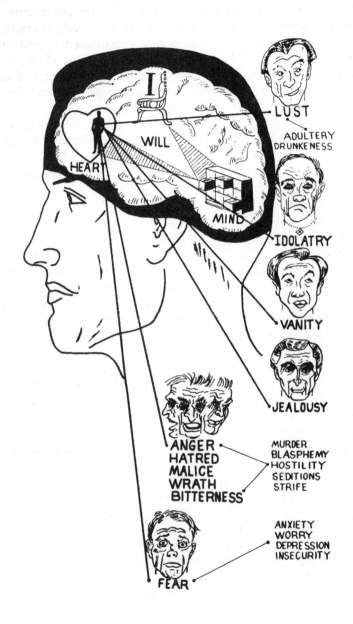

Dr. McMillen states, "The emotional center produces these widespread changes by means of three principal mechanisms: by changing the amount of blood flowing to an organ; by affecting the secretions of certain glands; and by changing the tension of muscles."[3] He then points out that the emotions of anger or hatred can cause the blood vessels to dilate, permitting an abnormal supply of blood to the head. The cranium is a rigid structure without room for expansion; consequently, anger and wrath can very easily give a person severe headaches.

A doctor friend illustrated the way in which our emotions can cause ulcers and many other stomach diseases by restricting the flow of blood to the stomach and other vital organs. He doubled up his fist until his knuckles turned white and said, "If I could keep my fist doubled up long enough, I would lose all feeling in my fingers, because the flow of blood has been restricted. The solution to that problem is very simple; all I have to do is relax." And with that he opened his hand and his fingers turned their normal color again. He said we have a muscle over our stomach that is emotionally controlled, and in a fit of rage it will tighten down and restrict the flow of blood to the vital organs of heart, stomach, liver, intestines, lungs, gallbladder, etc.

It is easy to see from this illustration that prolonged anger, resentment, hatred, wrath or bitterness could cause severe damage to these organs of the body. Dr. McMillen lists over 51 diseases which are caused by emotional stress. He even suggests that some very common infectious diseases are contracted when the resistance is low at the time of exposure, the reason being that prolonged emotional stress can reduce our resistance. Think of the needless sicknesses because of emotional stress of Christians who could have avoided all that heartache if they had been "filled with the Holy Spirit."

That answers for me the question that has been asked many times by rebellious, bitter Christians: "Why has God permitted all this sickness to come into my life?" It seems from the above and other medical findings that in most cases God didn't "permit" it; personal anger—sin—caused it.

Many a doctor has been forced to tell heart patients, victims of high blood pressure, sufferers of colitis, goiter and many other common diseases: "We can find nothing organically wrong with you; your problem is emotionally induced." Usually the patient will become angry because he thinks the doctor means, "It's all in your mind." What the doctor means is "It's all in your emotional center." One psychologist told me that he would estimate as many as 97 percent of the people who come to him with ulcers have them because of anger. In fact, one of his first questions on hearing a patient has ulcers is, "Who are you mad at?" He added, "Then they usually get mad at me."

The increase in physical illnesses originating from our emotions has given rise to the use of tranquilizers and other emotion-depressants. These treatments are very limited in their lasting effect because they do not deal with the cause of the problem. Psychologists tell us that man is not able to fully control his emotions even by his will. I agree, for I have found that nothing short of the power of Jesus Christ is able to make an angry, bitter, vitriolic individual loving, compassionate, gentle and kind. The cure for this problem through Jesus Christ will be given in chapter 10.

D. Spiritually

The highest price of all paid for an angry, bitter disposition is in the spiritual realm. Jesus Christ came to give us not only eternal life when we die, but abundant life here and now. That life can only be experienced by "abiding in Him" or "being filled with the Spirit." No man can abide in Christ or be filled with the Spirit who grieves the Holy Spirit, and "anger, bitterness, wrath, clamor and enmity of heart" grieve the Holy Spirit of God.

Grieving the Holy Spirit limits the work of God in an individual's life, keeps him from becoming mature in Christ Jesus, and hinders him from being the glowing, effective, fruitful Christian that he wants to be. Churches are filled today with evangelical Christians just like the children of Israel, who never fully possessed their possessions. Continual grieving of the Spirit of God through anger keeps the child of God from enjoying all that Jesus Christ has for him today. This affects the believer not only in this life but in the life to come, for we should be occupying ourselves with laying up treasures in heaven, which can be done only as we walk in the Spirit. Again we say, the most important single thing to any Christian is that he walk in the Spirit, but to do so he must let God cure his natural weakness of inner anger and turmoil.

The Basic Cause of Anger

What causes a perfectly normal, likeable, congenial human being to suddenly react with heat and anger? The full realization and acceptance of the answer to that question provides the Christian with his first giant step toward its cure. Stripped of all the facade and fancy excuses for condoning anger, of calling it "old nick" or "my natural Irish disposition," we are confronted with an ugly word—*selfishness*. Although we love to excuse our weaknesses and justify them to ourselves as we nurse our grudges and indulge in angry, vengeful, bitter feelings, they are all motivated by selfishness. When I am angry, it is because someone has violated my rights and I am interested in myself. When I am bitter against someone, it is because they have done something against me, and again I come back to selfishness. Vengeance is always inspired by selfishness.

A lovely Christian lady came to my study to tell me her side of the problems in her home. When I confronted her with the fact of her angry, bitter spirit, she blurted out in her defense, "Well, you'd be angry too if you lived with a man who constantly ran roughshod over you and treated you like dirt!" Admittedly, he was not treating her the way a Christian man should, but her reaction could not possibly be caused by generosity; instead, it was plain old selfishness. The more she indulged in her selfishness and let anger predominate, the worse her husband treated her.

I confronted her with the fact that she had two problems. She looked at me rather startled and asked, "Did I hear you correctly—I have two problems? I only have one, my husband." "No," I said, "you have two problems. Your husband is one problem, but your attitude toward your husband is another. Until you as a Christian recognize your own sin of selfishness and look to God for a proper attitude, even in the face of these circumstances, you will continue to grieve the Holy Spirit of God." The change in that woman in almost one month's time was almost unbelievable. Instead of using her husband as an excuse to indulge in anger, she began to treasure her relationship to Jesus Christ more than the indulgence of her own selfishness. She went to Him who has promised to "supply all your needs according to His riches in glory by Christ Jesus" and began to experience victory over bitterness, wrath, anger, and all those emotional attitudes that grieved the Holy Spirit. Instead of waiting for a change in her husband's behavior, she literally changed her husband's behavior by hers. She told me that when God gave her victory over her own reaction to his miserable disposition, she began being kind to the one who was "despitefully using her," just as our Lord had instructed. Since love begets love and we reap what we sow, it was not long before the husband began to respond with kindness.

As fantastic as it may seem, I have observed this in the lives of those individuals who are willing to recognize inner anger and turmoil as the sin of selfishness and look to God for the grace, love, and self-control which He promises to them who ask Him. It you are reaping a crop of anger, bitterness and hatred, a little investigation will indicate to you that you have been *sowing* a crop of anger, bitterness and hatred. The Bible tells us, "Whatsoever a man soweth, that shall he also reap." If you had been sowing love, you would be reaping love. If you are not reaping love, may I suggest that you change the seeds you are sowing.

REFERENCES

1. Raymond L. Cramer, *The Psychology of Jesus and Mental Health,* © 1959, Cowman Publications, Inc. page 27, used by permission.
2. S. I. McMillen, *None of These Diseases,* © Fleming H. Revell Comany, page 73, used by permission.
3. Ibid., page 60.

CHAPTER 9

Quenching The Holy Spirit Through Fear

> "Rejoice evermore.
> "Pray without ceasing.
> "In everything give thanks: for this is the will of God
> in Christ Jesus concerning you.
> "Quench not the Spirit."   (I Thessalonians 5:16-19)

Quenching and grieving the Holy Spirit are the two sins one must guard against in order to maintain the Spirit-filled life. We have already seen that one grieves the Holy Spirit through anger. We shall now see that we quench the Holy Spirit through fear. Quenching the Holy Spirit is stifling or limiting Him. Neither grieving nor quenching the Holy Spirit eliminates Him from our life, but they do seriously restrict His control of our body which God would otherwise strengthen and use.

Our text indicates that the Spirit-filled Christian should be one who is able to "rejoice . . . always" (Philippians 4:4) and "in everything give thanks." (I Thessalonians 5:18) Anytime the Christian does not rejoice or give thanks in everything, he is out of the will of God. That does not mean only in good circumstances, for even the natural man rejoices in enjoyable circumstances. But when the Scripture tells us "rejoice evermore" and "in everything give thanks," it means in any circumstance. Therefore, in order for man to give thanks for everything, he must live by faith. It is faith in God's love, God's power and God's plan for our lives that keeps us rejoicing through the Spirit in whatever circumstances we may find ourselves. An unhappy, unthankful attitude that quenches the

Holy Spirit is caused by unbelief in the faithfulness of our God, which produces fear as we face the uncertain circumstances of life. Thus I would have you examine the subject of quenching the Holy Spirit through fear.

Fear Is Universal

The first reaction to the sin of disobedience on the part of Adam and Eve was one of fear. When Adam and Eve "heard the voice of the Lord God walking in the garden in the cool of the day . . . Adam and his wife hid themselves from the presence of the Lord God amongst the trees in the garden. And the Lord God called unto Adam and said unto him, where art thou? And he said, I heard Thy voice in the garden and I was afraid because I was naked and I hid myself." (Genesis 3:8-10)

From that day to this the further man goes in disobedience to God, the more he experiences fear. The converse is also true. The more man obeys God, learns about God and leans upon Him for every need, the less he experiences fear. The universal nature of fear is easily seen in the fact that the Lord Jesus Himself so frequently admonished His disciples with such phrases as "fear not, little flock," "be not faithless, but believing," "O ye of little faith," and "Let not your heart be troubled, neither let it be afraid." Never in the history of the world has the universal problem of fear gripped so many and caused such devastation in the minds and bodies of men as the day in which we live. World conditions are not conducive to peace and faith today, for they cause many to lose their moorings and be afraid. The news media in our country constantly remind us of brutalities, wars, fightings, riotings, rapings and all kinds of frightful behavior. There is very little in the average daily newspaper that calms the emotions, but much that will turn man's natural fears into terror. In addition, there is what former President Kennedy referred to as the "Damocles sword" constantly hanging over our heads in the form of a nuclear holocaust.

It is comforting for the child of God, in the face of such fear reaction to world conditions, to heed the words of the Lord Jesus Christ who said, "Ye shall hear of wars and rumors of wars: *see that ye be not troubled.*" (Matthew 24:6) Even though fear is universal, God's children *do not* have to be dominated by this vicious emotional destroyer.

Reader's Digest for October, 1964, carried a popular reprint by Joseph Fort Newton, former pastor of St. James Church, Philadelphia, entitled "A Minister's Mail." He stated: "For some years I conducted a newspaper feature, 'Everyday Living,' which reached millions of people. Out of the mountains of letters not more than half a dozen ever brought up any question of theology, such as the differences which divide the religious communions. The first thing that these letters show is that Private Enemy No. 1 in human life is neither sin nor sorrow; it is fear. The one most rife is fear of ourselves, and that is not healthy. Men today fear failure, breakdown, poverty, fear lest they be unequal to the demands made upon them. So few have any material security; and we have set so much store by such security that the lack of it assumes hideous forms and gigantic dimensions in the night, robbing us of the rest needed to do our work aright. It is this self-fear which makes life an agony. Next to fear—if not a form of it—is the nagging, gnawing worry which wears us out and unfits us for living. Worry is a tiny rivulet seeping into the mind like slow poison, until it paralyzes us. Unless it is checked, it cuts a channel into which all other thoughts are drained."[1]

Fear, like anger, takes many forms. The accompanying chart describes the main variations.

An entire book could be devoted to this subject alone, but we shall limit ourselves to four categories.

The Emotional Cost of Fear

Every year countless thousands of individuals fall into mental and emotional collapse because of fear. Electric shock treatments and insulin shock treatments are becoming more and more common as forms of treatment to patients suffering from the tyrannical force of fear. Many a fearful person draws into a shell and lets life pass him by, never experiencing the rich things that God has in store for him, simply because he is afraid. The tragedy of it all is that most of the things he fears never happen. A young businessman addressing a sales company somehow came up with the figure that 92 percent of the

Expressions of Fear

Anxiety	Worry
Doubts	Inferiority
Timidity	Cowardice
Indecision	Suspicion
Superstition	Hesitancy
Withdrawal	Depression
Loneliness	Haughtiness
Overaggression	Social Shyness

things people fear will occur never take place. I cannot attest to the accuracy of his figure, but it is obvious in looking at anyone's life that the overwhelming majority of the things that cause our fear do not take place or are not nearly as severe as we thought they would be.

I counseled a woman who ten years before drove her husband from her because she was so emotionally upset due to fear. She became obsessed with the idea that another woman was going to take her husband away from her, and her emotionally upset mind caused such erratic and abnormal behavior in the home that she drove her husband away from her, though the "other woman" never existed.

The emotional cost of fear is very clearly seen in the statement by Dr. S. I. McMillen. "About nine million Americans suffer from emotional and mental illness. As many hospital beds are filled by the mentally deranged as are occupied by all the medical and surgical patients combined. In fact, one out of every 20 Americans will have a psychotic disturbance severe enough to confine him in a hospital for the insane. Mental disease is indeed the nation's No. 1 health problem. What does it cost to take care of the patients in our mental hospitals? The annual cost is about one billion dollars. Besides, outside the asylums there are a vast number who do not need confinement but who are incapable of supporting themselves. They work little or not at all and constitute a great burden on the taxpayer."[2] This cost does not include the heartache and confusion in the families from which these patients are admitted to sanitariums and asylums. Mothers or fathers are left to raise children singlehandedly, and children often go untrained or uncared for as a result of emotional illness of one parent or the other.

The Social Cost of Fear

The social cost of fear is perhaps the easiest to bear, but it is expensive nonetheless. Fear-dominated individuals do not make enjoyable company. Their pessimistic and complaining spirit causes them to be shunned and avoided, thus further deepening their emotional disturbances. Many otherwise likeable and happy people are scratched off social lists and cause their companions to be equally limited simply because of ungrounded fears.

The Physical Cost of Fear

Fear, like anger, produces emotional stress, and we have already seen that medically speaking this accounts for two-thirds or more of all physical illness today.

Some of the diseases mentioned by Dr. McMillen are high blood pressure, heart trouble, kidney disease, goiter, arthritis, headaches, strokes and most of the same 51 illnesses which he listed as caused by anger. In illustrating the effect of fear upon the human heart, he quotes Dr. Roy R. Grinker, one of the medical directors of Michael Reese Hospital in Chicago. "This doctor states that anxiety places more stress on the heart than any other stimulus, including physical exercise and fatigue."[3] Dr. McMillen points out that fear causes a chemical reaction to take place in the human body, as illustrated when the saliva seems to be drained from our mouth as we stand up in a speech class to speak. Such a reaction does not harm a person, because it is shortlived, but that type of experience indulged in hour after hour because of fear can cause physical damage to the body.

A doctor friend explained it to me in this way. We have an automatic alarm bell system that rings whenever we are confronted with an emergency. If the door bell rings at 2 a.m., you are awakened suddenly and in complete control of your faculties, no matter how sound a sleeper you happen to be. This is God's natural gift to the human being. What has happened is that your adrenal gland has been triggered by the fright of the emergency and has secreted adrenalin into your bloodstream, causing you to be immediately in control of all your faculties; in fact, you will probably be stronger and more mentally alert than normally so that you might adequately cope with the problem.

When I pastored a country church in South Carolina, one of the men of the congregation was speeding his expectant wife to the hospital to be delivered of her child. As they came down the muddy mountain road, the front of the car slipped into the ditch. In the face of the emergency his adrenal gland pumped adrenalin into his system; he leaped around in front of the car and literally slid it back up onto the road, got back into the car and drove his wife to the hospital. The next day in the parking lot of the hospital he tried to prove to incredulous friends that he had lifted the front of his Model A Ford, but to his amazement he could not budge it one inch. He used every ounce of energy and strength at his command, but the car would not move. What he didn't understand was that he had possessed super-normal strength because of his God-given emergency alarm system the night before that was not available for the parking lot demonstration.

My doctor friend explained that this does not cause any damage to the human body because after the emergency is over the adrenal gland settles down to its normal function and the bloodstream throws off the excessive adrenalin chemical with no ill effects. That is not the case, however, of the man who sits down at one o'clock in the afternoon to pay his bills and suddenly is overcome with fear because he does not have enough money in his checking account to pay for everything he owes. Hour after hour, as long as he worries, his adrenal gland is pumping adrenalin into his bloodstream, a process which can ultimately create much physical damage. This is sometimes the cause of excessive calcium deposits, and it sometimes produces the pain-racked bodies of arthritis sufferers.

I know a lovely Christian lady who has been afflicted with arthritis and was finally restricted by the disease to a wheelchair. She had every medical treatment known to science and was finally told by her third arthritis specialist, "I'm sorry, Mrs. ————, but we can find nothing organically wrong with you. The cause of your arthritis is emotional." When I heard that analysis, my mind went back to my childhood when she was in perfect health. Even though we enjoyed going to her house for the delicious cookies that she baked, we referred to her as "the professional worrier." She worried about everything. She fretted over her husband's employment, and he worked 30 years for the same company and never knew a day without pay. She was apprehensive about the future of a daughter who today has a lovely home and five children. She was anxious about her weak, sickly son who grew up to be a 6 foot-4 inch, 225-pound tackle for a Big Ten football team. I can hardly think of anything she didn't worry about, and all to no avail.

No wonder the Lord Jesus said in His Sermon on the Mount, "Take no thought for your life, what ye shall eat, or what ye shall drink; nor yet for your body, what ye shall put on. . . ." (Matthew 6:25) Literally, that is "take no anxious thought." Again the Holy Spirit tells us, "Be anxious for nothing." (Philippians 4:6) Anxiety and worry which stem from fear cause untold physical suffering, limitations and premature death not only to non-Christians, but also to Christians who disobey the admonition to: "commit thy way unto the Lord and trust also in Him." (Psalms 37:5)

One day I called upon what I thought was an older woman who was bedridden. I was amazed to find that she was 15-20 years younger than I had estimated. She made herself old before her time by being a professional worrier. As gently and yet as truthfully as I could, I tried to show her that she should learn to trust the Lord and not worry about everything. Her reaction was so typical it bears repeating. With fire in her eye and a flash of anger in her voice she asked, "Well, someone has to worry about things, don't they?" "Not if you have a heavenly Father who loves you and is interested in every detail of your life," I replied. But that dear sister didn't get the point. I hope you do!

Thank God we are not orphans! We live in a society that accepts the concept that we are the products of a biological accident and a long unguided process of evolution. That popular theory, which is rapidly falling into scientific disrepute, is not only incorrect but is enslaving mankind in a prison house of physical torture due to fear. If you are a Christian, memorize Philippians 4:6, 7, and every time you find yourself worrying or becoming anxious, pray. Thank God that you have a heavenly Father who is interested in your problems, and turn them over to Him. Your little shoulders are not broad enough to carry the weight of the world or even your own family problems, but the Lord Jesus "is able to do exceeding abundantly above all that we ask or think." (Ephesians 3:20)

How thrilled I was recently when a little girl in our Beginners Department quoted her memory verse for me. She said, "I learned in Sunday school today what God wants me to do with my problems. For He said, 'Casting all your care upon Him; for He careth for you,' I Peter 5:7." Much of the physical suffering and consequent heartache, including financial difficulties, that occur in the average Christian home would be avoided if believers really acted upon that verse.

The Spiritual Cost of Fear

The spiritual cost of fear is very similar to the spiritual cost of anger. It quenches or stifles the Holy Spirit, which keeps us from being effective in this life and steals many of our rewards in the life to come. Fear keeps us from being joyful, happy, radiant Christians and instead makes us thankless, complaining, defeated Christians who are unfaithful. A fearful person is not going to manifest the kind of life that encourages a sinner to come to him and say, "Sir, what must I do to be saved?" If Paul and Silas had let their fears predominate, the Philippian jailer would never have been converted and we would not have the great salvation verse, Acts 16:31.

Fear keeps the Christian from pleasing God. The Bible tells us, "Without faith it is impossible to please God." (Hebrews 11:6) The eleventh chapter of Hebrews, which is called the "Faith Chapter," names men whose biography is given in sufficient detail throughout the Scriptures to establish that they represent all four of the basic temperament types. The thing that made these men acceptable in the sight of God is that they were not overcome by their natural weakness of either fear or anger, but walked with God by faith. Consider these four men representative of the four temperament types: Peter the Sanguine, Paul the Choleric, Moses the Melancholy and Abraham the Phlegmatic. It is difficult to find more dynamic illustrations of the power of God working in the lives of men than these four. "God is no respecter of persons." What He did to strengthen their weaknesses He will do through His Holy Spirit for you!

What Causes Fear?

Because fear is such a universal experience of man and because most of the readers of this book will be parents who can help their children avoid this tendency, I would like to answer this question simply in layman's terms. There are at least eight causes of fear.

1. Temperament traits

We have already seen that the melancholy and phlegmatic temperaments are indecisive and fear-prone. Although Mr. Sanguine is not nearly as self-confident as his blustering way would have us believe, he too can become fearful. Very few cholerics would not have some melancholy or phlegmatic tendencies, so that conceivably all people will have a temperament tendency toward fear, though some more than others.

2. Childhood experiences

Psychologists and psychiatrists agree that the basic needs of man are love, understanding and acceptance. The most significant human thing that parents can do for their children—short of leading one's children to a saving knowledge of Jesus Christ—is to give them the warmth and security of parental love. This does not exclude discipline or the teaching of submission to standards and principles. In fact, it is far better for a child to learn to adjust to rules and standards in the loving atmosphere of his home than in the cruel world outside. There are, however, two specific parental habits I suggest you diligently avoid:

Over-protection. An over-protective parent makes a child self-centered and fearful of the very things happening to him that his parent is afraid will happen. Children quickly learn to read our emotions. Their bodies can far more easily absorb the falls, burns and shocks of life than their emotions can absorb our becoming tense, upset or hysterical over these minor experiences. The fearful mother that forbids her son to play football probably does far more harm to his emotional development by her repeated suggestions of fear than the damage done to Junior if his front teeth were knocked out or his leg broken. Legs heal and teeth can be replaced, but it takes a miracle of God to remove the scar tissues of fear from our emotions.

Dominating children. Angry, explosive parents who dominate the lives of their children or who critically pounce upon every failure in their lives often create hesitancy, insecurity and fear in them. Children need correction, but they need it done in the proper spirit. Whenever we have to point out our children's mistakes, we should also make it a practice to note their strengths and good points, or at least criticize them in such a way as to let them know that they are still every bit as much the object of our love as they were before.

The more I counsel with people, the more convinced I am that the most devastating blow one human being can inflict upon another is *disapproval.* The more a person loves us, the more important it is for us to seek some area in his life where we can show our approval. A 6-foot-2 inch husband in the midst of marriage counseling said rather proudly, "Pastor, I have never laid a hand on my wife in anger!" As I looked at his timid, cowering, 110 pound wife, I knew by the look in her eye what she was thinking: "Well, I would a thousand times rather that you beat me physically than constantly run me down and club me with disapproval."

The Spirit-filled parent is inspired through his loving, compassionate nature to build others up and to show approval whenever possible. Even in the times of correction he will convey his love. To do otherwise with our children is to leave lasting fear-scars on their emotions.

3. A traumatic experience

Child assault or molesting leaves a lasting emotional scar that often carries over into adulthood, causing fear concerning the act of marriage. Other tragic experiences in childhood frequently set fear-patterns into motion that last throughout life.

During the past few years our family has enjoyed some wonderful occasions water skiing. The only member of the family that has not tried it is my wife, and she is deathly afraid of the water. I have begged her, encouraged her and done everything I could to entice her to get over this fear of the water, but to no avail. Finally last summer I gave up. She made one Herculean attempt to overcome this fear by donning a wetsuit that could easily sustain her body in water. She then put on a life jacket, which also by itself could sustain her in water, and very hesitantly lowered herself over the side of the boat. The moment her hand left the security of the boat and she was floating freely in the water, I noted a look of terror in her eyes. For the first time I really understood how frightened she was of the water. Upon questioning her, I found that it all went back to a childhood experience in Missouri when she came within an eyelash of drowning. These experiences leave hidden marks on a person's emotions that often follow them through life.

4. A negative thinking pattern

A negative thinking pattern or defeatist complex will cause a person to be fearful of attempting any new thing. The moment we start suggesting to ourselves "I can't, I can't, I can't" we are almost certain of failure. Our mental attitude makes even ordinary tasks difficult to perform when we approach them with a negative thought. Repeated failures or refusal to do what our contemporaries are able to accomplish often causes further breakdown in self-confidence and increases fear. A Christian need never be dominated by this negative habit. By memorizing Philippians 4:13 and seeking the Spirit's power in applying it, one can gain a positive attitude toward life.

5. Anger

Anger, as pointed out in the previous chapter, can produce fear. I have counseled with individuals who had indulged bitterness and anger until they erupted in such explosive tirades that they afterward admitted, "I'm afraid of what I might do to my own child."

6. Sin produces fear

"If our heart condemn us not, then have we confidence toward God" (I John 3:21) is a principle that cannot be violated without producing fear. Every time we sin, our conscience reminds us of our relationship to God. This has often been misconstrued by psychiatrists who blame religion for creating guilt complexes in people which, they said, in turn produced fear. A few years ago our family doctor, who at that time was not a Christian, made the following statement to me: "You ministers, including my saintly old father, do irreparable damage to the emotional life of men by preaching the gospel." I questioned his reason for such a statement and he said, "I took my internship in a mental institution, and the overwhelming majority of those people had a religious background and were there because of fear induced by guilt complexes."

The next day I attended a ministers' meeting where Dr. Clyde Narramore, a Christian psychologist from Los Angeles, gave a lecture on pastoral counseling. During the question period I told him of the previous day's conversation and asked his opinion. Dr. Narramore instantly replied: "That is not true. People have guilt complexes because they are guilty!" The result of sin is a consciousness of guilt, and guilt causes fear in modern man just as it did to Adam and Eve in the Garden of Eden. A simple remedy for this is: "Walk in the way of the Lord."

7. Lack of faith

Lack of faith, even in a Christian's life, can produce fear. I have noticed in counseling that fear caused by lack of faith is basically confined to two common areas.

The first is fear concerning the sins of the past. Because the Christian does not know what the Bible teaches in relationship to confessed sin, he has not come to really believe that God has cleansed him from all sin. (I John 1:9) Sometime ago I counseled with a lady who was in such a protracted period of fear that she had sunk into deep depression. We found that one of her basic problems was that she was still haunted by a sin committed 11 years before. All during this time she had been a Christian but had gone through a complete emotional collapse, haunted by the fear of that past sin.

When I asked if she had confessed that sin in the name of Jesus Christ, she replied, "Oh, yes, many times." I then gave her a spiritual prescription to make a Bible study of all Scripture verses that deal with the forgiveness of sins. When she came back into my office two weeks later, she was not the same woman. For the first time in her life she really understood how God regarded her past sin, and when she began to agree with Him that it was "remembered against her no more," she got over that fear.

A man I counseled who had a similar problem gave me a slightly different answer when I asked, "Have you confessed that sin to Christ?" "Over a thousand times," was his interesting reply. I told him that was 999 times too many. He should have confessed it once and thanked God 999 times that He had forgiven him for that awful sin. The Word of God is the cure for this problem, because "Faith cometh by hearing, and hearing by the Word of God." (Romans 10:17)

The second area in which men are prone to be fearful because of lack of faith concerns the future. If the devil can't get them to worry about their past sins, he will seek to get them to worry about God's provision in the future, and thus they are not able to enjoy the riches of God's blessing today. The Psalmist has said, "This is the day which the Lord hath made; we will rejoice and be glad in it." (Psalm 118:24) People who enjoy life are not "living tomorrow" nor worrying about the past; they are living today.

Anyone who thinks about the potential problems and difficulties he might encounter tomorrow will naturally become fearful unless he has a deep, abiding faith in God's ability to supply all his need. My wife shared with me a very beautiful saying she heard which bears repeating: "Satan tries to crush our spirit by getting us to bear tomorrow's problems with only today's grace."

If you are worrying about tomorrow, you can't possibly enjoy today. The interesting thing is that you can't give God tomorrow; you can only give Him what you have, and you have today. Dr. Cramer quoted a comment by Mr. John Watson in the Houston Times which read:

"What does your anxiety do? It does not empty tomorrow of its sorrow, but it empties today of its strength. It does not make you escape the evil; it makes you unfit to cope with it if it comes."[4]

Now I think you are about ready to face the primary cause of fear. The above seven causes of fear are only contributing factors. The basic cause for fear is . . .

8. Selfishness—the basic cause of fear

As much as we don't like to face this ugly word, it is a fact nonetheless. We are fearful because we are selfish. Why am I afraid? Because I am interested in self. Why am I embarrassed when I stand before an audience? Because I don't wish to make a fool of myself. Why am I afraid I will lose my job? Because I am afraid of being a failure in the eyes of my family or not being able to provide my family and myself with the necessities of life. Excuse it if you will, but all fear can be traced basically to the sin of selfishness.

Don't Be a Turtle

A Christian woman went to a Christian psychologist and asked, "Why am I so fearful?" He asked several questions. "When you enter a room, do you feel that everyone is looking at you?" "Yes," she said. "Do you often have the feeling your slip is showing?" "Yes." When he discovered she played the piano he asked, "Do you hesitate to volunteer to play the piano at church for fear someone else can do so much better?" "How did you know?" was her reply. "Do you hesitate to entertain others in your home?" Again she said, "Yes." Then he proceeded to tell her kindly that she was a very selfish young woman. "You are like a turtle," he said. "You pull into your shell and peek out only as far as necessary. If anyone gets too close, you pop your head back inside your shell for protection. That shell is selfishness. Throw it away and start thinking more about others and less about yourself."

The young lady went back to her room in tears. She never thought of herself as selfish, and it crushed her when she was confronted with the awful truth. Fortunately, she went to God, and He has gradually cured her of that vicious sin. Today she is truly a "new creature." She entertains with abandon, has completely thrown off the old "shell," and consequently enjoys a rich and abundant life.

Who Wants To Be an Oyster?

A similar statement is made by Dr. Maltz in his book, *Psycho-Cybernetics:* "One final word about preventing and removing emotional hurts. To live creatively, we must be willing to be a little vulnerable. We must be willing to be hurt a little, if necessary, in creative living. A lot of people need a thicker and tougher emotional skin than they have. But they need only a tough emotional hide or epidermis—not a shell. To trust, to love, to open ourselves to emotional communication with other people is to run the risk of being hurt. If we are hurt once, we can do one of two things. We can build a thick protective shell, or scar tissue, to prevent being hurt again, live like an oyster, and not be hurt. Or we can 'turn the other cheek,' remain vulnerable and go on living creatively.

"An oyster is never 'hurt.' He has a thick shell which protects him from everything. He is isolated. An oyster is secure, but not creative. He cannot 'go after' what he wants—he must wait for it to come to him. An oyster knows none of the hurts' of emotional communication with his environment—but neither can an oyster know the joys."[5]

Once fear has been faced as a sin rather than excused as a behavior pattern, the patient is well on the road to recovery provided he knows Jesus Christ and is willing to submit himself to the filling of the Holy Spirit. A more detailed cure for fear will be given in the chapter, "How to Overcome Your Weaknesses Through the Filling of the Holy Spirit."

REFERENCES
1. Joseph Fort Newton, "A Minister's Mail," *Reader's Digest* Reprint (October, 1964).
2. McMillen, op. cit., page 116.
3. Ibid., page 62.
4. Cramer, op. cit., page 28.
5. Maxwell Maltz, *Psycho-Cybernetics,* © Wilshire Book Co., pages 151-152, used by permission.

CHAPTER 10

Depression, Its Cause And Cure

A study of emotionally-induced illness would not be complete without a look at depression. Almost every one has known what it is to be depressed. During the last two years it has been my privilege to be in several churches speaking on family-life subjects in which I spend a night each on anger, fear and depression. I have made it a point the night before speaking on depression to ask the audience, "How many of you will honestly admit that at some time in your life you have been depressed?" To my knowledge every hand has been raised, attesting to the universal experience of depression.

Dr. Cramer, in his treatment of this subject, states: "Emotional depression is widespread if not almost universal. Severe depressed states have characterized human history ever since Adam's dejection following his expulsion from the Garden of Eden. Depression is an emotional illness to which many of our socially most useful and productive people are subject. Depressive traits cover a wide range of professional groups— the sophisticated and highly intelligent are not exempt!"[1]

Just being depressed does not mean that there is anything wrong with your intelligence . . . I have known people who had no education and those with Ph.D.'s alike depressed. I am acquainted with a man and his wife who are getting their Ph.D.'s in psychology at the same time, and they are both seriously depressed. Perhaps the fact that each has to live with a psychologist and be subject to perpetual analysis is enough to depress them!

Depression is defined by Webster's dictionary as "the state of being depressed . . . dejection, as of mind . . . a lowering of vitality of functional activity . . . an abnormal state of inactivity and unpleasant emotion." God never intended man to live like that! It has always been God's intent that man enjoy a peaceful, contented, and happy life, referred to in Scripture as the "abundant" life. No Christian filled with the Holy Spirit is going to be depressed. Before a Spirit-filled believer can become depressed, he must first grieve the Spirit through anger or quench the Spirit through fear. Before we examine the specific causes of depression, let us examine the heavy costs.

The High Cost of Being Depressed

Every negative human emotion indulged in over a period of time takes a heavy toll on a person. Depression is not just an emotional state, but the result of a particular thinking pattern which we shall discuss near the end of this chapter. But it too takes a heavy toll. Consider the following five costs as only part of the price one pays for depression, depending on how serious and prolonged it is.

1. Gloom and pessimism

When a person is depressed, he is gloomy and pessimistic. Everything looks black, and even the most simple things become difficult. It seems a common practice for a depressed person to "make a mountain out of a molehill." That does not make for good fellowship; consequently a depressed person is not sought out by his friends, and thus he tends to become more depressed. People do not seek the companionship of the depressed in spirit, but the lighthearted. Selfish motive? Yes, but true nevertheless. The gloomy, pessimistic spirit of the depressed person usually makes him a very lonely individual.

2. Apathy and fatigue

Another price paid by the depressed person is apathy and fatigue. These conditions, like anger and fear, involve very fatiguing emotions. It takes considerable energy to be angry all day or to lie awake worrying all night, and this expenditure of energy does not leave an angry or fear-dominated person with much pep to enjoy the pleasurable blessings of life. But depression is often worse than fear and anger in that it tends to neutralize man's natural ambitions. Since molehills look like mountains, his attitude usually is, "What's the use?" and he pessimistically sits on his stool of gloom and does nothing.

Man needs the sense of accomplishment that comes with a task well done. This feeling of well-being so needed by the depressed person is repelled by his apathy, which is the enemy of all achievement; it certainly is not the soil from which the seeds of "goals," "projects" and "visions" grow. The Bible tells us that "without a vision the people perish." That is true not only in the spiritual realm, but also in the mental realm. If people do not have a vision or goal to which they are working, mentally they are living in a vacuum of apathy that saps the vitality of their energy.

This lack of vision accounts for much of the apathetic behavior of young people today. Our society has overprotected them to the point that it has failed to challenge them. Now we have a growing generation on our hands that may not be willing to defend their country against an evil enemy like Communism. This attitude will carry over into many other areas of life, and with the increase in specialization it is going to be increasingly difficult to succeed in business and professional life. The younger generation needs greater motivation today than any preceding generation, but instead has less.

This indicates that we can expect an increase in depressed people. But thanks to God, there is victory from this depression through Jesus Christ our Lord. The rise in depressed individuals will increase the number of souls who will recognize their need of outside stimulus in seeking a cure. This fact should quicken the consciousness of Spirit-filled believers with the fact that all about them are apathetic, depressed, empty-hearted, no-vision souls that desperately need Christ. This is the most thrilling day the world has seen in several generations to live the Spirit-filled life as a demonstration of what Jesus Christ is able to do for an individual.

3. Hypochondria

Another problem occasioned by depression is hypochondria. A depressed person has aching pains, a sore stomach, and numerous difficulties without any known cause. He can learn the art of being sick to excuse his apathy. Some people use this "tool" to avoid what they think are unpleasant tasks by pretending to be sick. They don't call it pretending, or even think of it so, of course; it is very real to them, but usually unnecessary.

The ability of the human mind to cause physical pain is seen in the case a doctor friend of mine had recently. He has used hypnosis in his practice to deliver babies, calm the nervous, assist weight control, relieve tension caused by traumatic experiences and cure many other maladies. A golfer came in "to be hypnotized and have my trick elbow cured." It seems he had the "traumatic experience" of losing a championship golf match by seriously overputting the ninth cup. When he came to the 18th hole, he thought about it again, and his elbow seemed to hurt. Again he was overputting the cup. Ever since then his elbow ached whenever he picked up his putter, particularly when he came to the ninth or eighteenth green. Through hypnotic suggestion this "terrible pain" was eliminated.

In this same way aches and pains can enslave a depressed person any time he thinks of some unpleasant task or experience. Millions of dollars and untold human suffering are the price being paid for this hypochondria-type sickness induced by depression.

A healthy mental attitude toward things can hardly be overemphasized. I remember counseling with a housewife who "hated housework." She loved her home, children and husband but by her own testimony "hated to do dishes, and it irks me because my husband won't buy me a dishwasher." She had made a martyr of herself every time she stood at the kitchen sink. What was the problem? It was her attitude toward the doing of the dishes that made her sick. It was her attitude that made it an unpleasant, boring, exhausting task that almost destroyed the many other blessings which surrounded her but which she was overlooking. She was forgetting the lovely home, furniture, faithful husband and healthy children. Instead, she was focusing upon a pet peeve through the magnifying glass of self-interest. This is always a formula for depression.

Actually, a degree of stress created by tackling a difficult task, or one we think difficult, is good for a person, presupposing a positive mental attitude toward it. Dr. McMillen has said, "I can recall many times having to make house calls on patients when I wasn't feeling well myself. I found out that the stress of making the trip often cured me of my minor aches and pains. However, if I had made the trip in the spirit of antagonism, my faulty reaction might have put me in the hospital for a week. Is it not a remarkable fact that our reactions to stress determine whether stress is going to cure us or make us sick? Here is an important key to longer and happier living. We hold the key and can decide whether stress is going to work for us or against us. Our attitude decides whether stress makes us 'better or bitter'."[2]

4. Loss of Productivity

It is only natural that if depression leads to apathy, then it also leads to loss of productivity. Many a genius or gifted individual never realizes his potential because of his depression-induced apathy. The loss is not only in this life, but also in the life to come. (See I Corinthians 3:10-15) The Lord Jesus' parable in Matthew 25:14-30 pointed out this very thing. He pictured his return as a time for his servants' accounting, and He seriously rebuked one for being "a wicked and slothful servant." He had not murdered anyone nor committed adultery; he had merely done nothing with the talent our Lord gave him. Some Christians are going to lose rewards in this life and the life to come because they are doing nothing with the talents the Lord has given them.

Apathy produces apathy just as depression produces depression. Christians tend to become depressed and apathetic if their lives do not count for Christ. Repeatedly taking in the Word of God without expressing it to other souls has a tendency to make one depressively apathetic. Recently a young Christian that has had a problem with depression most of his life said, "Last Friday I felt wonderful! I had a great opportunity to witness my faith to a fellow employee." There is tremendous therapy in witnessing our faith to other people.

5. Irritability

A person suffering from depression is prone to be irritable. It irritates him that others are in a good, energetic mood when he is in a pensive, gloomy mood. He is also irritated by petty things that would otherwise completely escape his attention.

6. Withdrawal

Severe cases of depression lead to withdrawal. The individual tends to escape from the unpleasant realities of life, daydreaming about his pleasant childhood (which may at this point be a figment of his imagination) or building air castles about the future. This is very natural since contemplation of the present is depressing. Daydreaming, however, is a serious deterrent to an effective thinking process and not at all beneficial to mental health. It also makes a person uncommunicative and isolated.

The Cause of Depression

Since depression is a universal experience, it is worth our time to examine its basic causes. I will give the standard suggested causes and then turn to the most common cause.

Temperament tendencies

Although depression is common to all temperament types, there is none that is so vulnerable to this problem as the melancholy temperament. Mr. Melancholy can go into longer and deeper periods of depression than any of his fellows. Mr. Sanguine can be depressed for a brief period of time, but since he is so susceptible to his immediate environment, he experiences a change of mood as soon as he has a change of environment. Thus a cheerful companion coming on the scene can transform his mood of depression into one of joy.

Mr. Choleric is a perennial optimist, and he looks with such disdain upon depression because of its impractical resultant apathy that he does not ordinarily become a slave to it. He is not overly occupied with himself, but has long-range goals and plans which more than occupy his mind in the field of productivity, which is not conducive to depression. Mr. Phlegmatic would probably rate second in depressive tendencies among the four temperament types, though his periods of depression would not be as frequent nor as deep as the melancholy because of his basically cheerful nature and his sense of humor. It should be borne in mind, however, that we are not one solid temperament type; therefore, if a person is predominantly phlegmatic with some melancholy tendencies, he is going to be vulnerable to depression. Or if he is a combination of choleric with some melancholy, again he will experience depression. Thus we see why it is imperative to understand the universal aspect of depression.

There are three reasons why Mr. Melancholy has the problem of depression more than others.

1. His greatest weakness is self-centeredness. Everything in his life is related to self. He spends a great deal of his time in self-examination. Dr. D. Martyn Lloyd-Jones states the following: "The fundamental trouble with these people is that they are not always careful to draw the line of demarcation between self-examination and introspection. We all agree that we should examine ourselves, but we also agree that introspection and morbidity are bad. But what is the difference between examining oneself and becoming introspective? I suggest that we cross the line from self-examination to introspection when, in a sense, we do nothing but examine ourselves, and when such self-examination becomes the main and chief end in our life."[3] Essentially, then, the difference is that self-examination is commendable when it results in doing something about that which has been discovered. Self-examination for its own sake is introspection, which produces depression.

2. Mr. Melancholy is a perfectionist; therefore, he finds it easy to criticize not only others, but himself. No person can become so distressed with his own work as Mr. Melancholy. The fact that it is far better than that of the other temperament types means nothing to him. That it does not measure up to his supreme standard of perfection bothers him and causes him to become depressed at what he considers his own failure.

Psychologists tell us that a melancholy person is often prone to be over-conscientious. Dr. Cramer expresses it this way: "The depressive takes life too seriously. He has a narrow range of interests, develops a meticulous devotion to duty, and is preoccupied with the smallest, most insignificant details. Combined with these traits there is often a compelling drive for the highest possible degree of success and excellence. The depressed person can put out a surprising amount of constructive work and assume a great deal of responsibility. He accomplishes this by driving himself ruthlessly. He is a slavedriver for getting results; he brags of his accomplishments, prides himself that his work cannot be duplicated, that no one else could possibly take his place, that his efforts are indispensable; his drive for power and control, his lack of appreciation for the feelings of others make him almost impossible to get along with."[4] Thus we see that even when he reaches his standard of perfection, he can become disagreeable, unlovable, and unappreciated which throws him into a fit of depression.

3. A perfectionist has a tendency to be unrealistic, both toward himself and others. He seems incapable of adjusting to the demands made upon him by changes in the course of life. For instance, a very active person at church—one who teaches a Sunday school class, directs youth groups, and is active in the calling program—may not recognize that duties at home also demand his attention. Certainly the standard of Christian service at church is higher for the single person or young married couple without children than for a young mother with three small children. Home responsibilities, of course, should not be offered as an excuse for lack of church attendance, but the curtailment of some Christian activities should not cause Mrs. Melancholy to feel that she is forsaking her spiritual service, or that she is a success as a mother but a failure as a Christian. The truth of the matter is, she is not a success as a Christian until she is a success as a mother.

The person who already has an overloaded schedule must either neglect his family or shirk some responsibility (which makes the perfectionists guilt-stricken) when taking on additional duties. Happy is the man who knows his limitations and refuses to accept another responsibility unless he can complete the one for which he is presently accountable. It is far better to do a good job of a few things than a poor job of many things. This is particularly true of a conscientious person with perfectionist tendencies, for unless he does his best, he will never be satisfied with his accomplishments. Dissatisfaction with one's accomplishments often leads to depression.

Hypocrisy leads to depression

The average Christian who attends a Bible-teaching church soon learns the standards of the Christian life. If he attacks his weaknesses externally rather than by the control of the Holy

Spirit working from within, he may become depressed. Suppose a man has a problem with resentment, bitterness and hostility. He soon learns that this is not the standard of spirituality for the Christian. Unless he handles this matter on a personal basis with God, he will try to solve it by the power of self-control. To control anger by the force of one's will is not only futile, but it will lead to an explosion somewhere in the body—high blood pressure, heart trouble, ulcers, colitis, or a myriad of other maladies, or it may result in a belated explosion. The frustration that follows an angry reaction to a given situation leads to depression. A true cure for these problems will be dealt with in detail in the next chapter. Suffice it to say here that it must come from within through the power of the Holy Spirit.

Physical problems

Physical problems can lead to depression. Whenever a person is weak, even simple difficulties are magnified. This can be avoided in physical weakness when one bears in mind the principle given by the Apostle Paul in II Corinthians 12:9-10, "When I am weak, then am I strong." Paul knew that the grace of God is sufficient for a Christian after a severe illness or at any other time in his Christian experience.

I have observed that individuals can become depressed when there is a mineral or vitamin deficiency. I am told that Vitamin B is the nerve vitamin, the complete absence of which can make a person nervous, which in turn may lead to frustration and depression. It is also apparent that some women suffer a hormone deficiency when going through the change of life, and this deficiency often produces depression. Before a person attributes all of his depression to spiritual reasons, physical causes should be investigated by his physician; however, most people are inclined to attribute their depression to physical problems rather than consider that it is spiritually and emotionally induced.

The Devil

Most Bible teachers remind us that the devil can oppress a Christian even if he does not indwell or possess him. It is true that some Christians have seemingly been depressed by the devil. Personally, I am not overly impressed with this reason because the Bible tells us, "He that is in you is greater than he that is in the world." Therefore, if a Christian is depressed by the devil, it is because he is not "abiding in Christ" or is not "filled with the Holy Spirit." We have already seen the nine characteristics of the Spirit-filled life. I do not find any place for depression as caused by the devil in the life of the Spirit-filled Christian. But it should be borne in mind that all Christians are not Spirit-filled. We must meet the conditions as outlined in that chapter and walk in the Spirit to avoid being depressed by the devil.

Rebellion and unbelief

The 79th Psalm shows the way in which Israel seriously limited God by their rebellious unbelief. God's limitation, because they refused to trust Him in their rebellion, caused them to be depressed with their circumstances. The terms "unbelief" and "rebellion" are used interchangeably in this instance, for unbelief leads to rebellion and rebellion leads to unbelief. If man really knew God as He is, he would believe Him implicitly. But because his faith is so weak, he has a tendency to rebel against the testings or the leading of the Lord, and rebellion and unbelief lead to depression.

Some years ago a very fine Christian worker came to me for counseling. She was already in the deep throes of apathy caused by depression. As I counseled with her, I found she was hostile toward many people, very bitter, and rebellious toward God. It seems that some well-meaning but ill-guided friend convinced her that they should have a special healing service for her that she might be "healed" of a lifelong illness. Such a meeting was held and she was declared "healed." She immediately discarded her medication and went around telling everyone of the marvelous work of God.

For some time she had no ill effects from the cessation of her medication, and then suddenly, without warning, she was gripped in the titanic vise of that lifelong disease. She returned to her doctor and resumed her medication, which arrested that problem. Nothing, however, has been invented to arrest the problem of rebellion (except acknowledging it as an awful sin and asking God to take it away). In the course of our counseling, she acknowledged that she was angry at God because He had not healed her the way she wanted Him to. She had not prayed in the will of God; instead, she had prayed in her own will, demanding that God answer her prayer exactly as she prescribed. Because He did not, she turned in unbelieving rebellion against Him, and in her frustration grew progressively depressed and apathetic. She refused to acknowledge her sin of rebellion and continued to prescribe her own cure for "healing this lifelong disease." She obviously was not aware that she had a far greater problem than her lifelong illness— namely, rebellion—and that God was using her sickness to help her realize her sin.

Instead of repenting of her sin by the simple method I prescribed and seeking God's grace to live with her illness (II Corinthians 12:9), she persisted in her rebellion. Today she is confined to a mental institution because her depression has become so severe she has lost touch with reality. This is a rare case, but it nevertheless illustrates that fact that rebellion leads to depression.

Psychological letdown

There is a natural psychological letdown whenever a great project has been completed. A very energetic and creative individual can be happy and contented while working toward a long-range goal. But when the goal is reached, it is often followed by a period of depression because the individual has not been able to mount another project to succeed the one he has concluded. This could well explain why many ministers leave their churches within six months after completing a building program. As I look back at my own life, I find that the only times I have had "itchy feet" and thought my ministry in a church finished was right after a long building program. Little did I realize that this was the natural reaction to the termination of a long-range project. The feeling of depression was eliminated when new projects and higher goals were set to replace those completed.

Elijah, the great prophet, had a similar experience after calling down fire from heaven and slaying 450 prophets of Baal. He sat down under a Juniper tree ". . . and he requested for himself that he might die; and said, it is enough; now, O Lord, take away my life; for I am not better than my fathers." (I Kings 19:4) This gifted prophet, unusually faithful to God, had strong melancholy tendencies, but because of the faithfulness of God he went on to greater heights of service for the Lord because he kept his eye on the goal of serving his Master.

Self-pity—the basic cause of depression

As important as they are, the above-mentioned elements are not the primary cause for depression. Too often they are the excuse one uses to condone depression rather than going to Almighty God for His marvelous cure. The truth of the matter is, a person becomes depressed only after a period of indulging in the sin of self-pity. I have questioned hundreds of individuals who were depressed and have yet to find an exception to this rule. I have had a number of people deny at the outset that self-pity was the cause, but upon thorough questioning they finally admitted that their thought-process prior to the period of depression was one of self-pity.

Dr. McMillen points out the many physical illnesses produced by the emotions of jealousy, envy, self-centeredness, ambition, frustration, rage, resentment, and hatred. He then observes: "These disease-producing emotions are concerned with protecting and coddling the self, and they could be summarized under one title—*self-centeredness.*"[4] He further states, "Chronic brooding over sorrows and insults indicates faulty adaptation, which can cause any condition from itching feet to insanity. The most common form of faulty reaction is *self-pity.*"[5]

The sin of self-pity is so subtle that we do not often recognize it for what it is. While I was holding meetings in a church some years ago, a very lovely Christian woman about 70 years of age came to me about her problem of "depression." This woman was a seemingly mature Christian lady with a gifted mind and many years of experience teaching an adult Bible class. She had been told by pastors of former churches, "You are the best woman Bible teacher I have ever known on a local church level," and it was apparent to me that she truly had a grasp of the Word of God.

At first I was at a loss to know how to reveal her self-pity to her, and I asked God secretly for special insight as she talked. It was not long until I found myself asking how she enjoyed her church, and her response immediately proved that I had "struck a nerve," for she said, "Nobody appreciates me around here! In fact, these people aren't very friendly. Most of the people in this church are young married couples, and they don't pay any attention to a widow like me. As far as they are concerned, I could quit coming to this church right now and they'd never miss me. They don't need me around here; in fact, I can come to this church on some Sundays and go away without anyone ever speaking to me."

There you have it! Depression caused by self-pity. Only when I wrote down those words that came from her own lips was I able to convince that dear woman that she had been indulging in the sin of self-pity, which caused her depression. I would be the first to acknowledge that self-pity is natural. But the Bible clearly teaches that we do not have to be dominated by the natural man, for we are to "walk in the Spirit." (Galatians 5:16)

One day I dropped in to see a minister friend of mine and his wife. While we were having a cup of coffee, the phone rang and the pastor went to answer it. As soon as he was out of earshot, his wife said, "I'd like to ask you something. Why is it that I have greater periods of depression today than when we were young in the ministry? Our work is going well, God is blessing, we have enough to live on, and yet I find that I go through more periods of depression now than when we had far greater problems."

Not wanting to ruin a good friendship, I reluctantly asked, "Are you sure you really want to know?" "Yes," she replied. "It isn't very pretty; in fact, it's rather ugly," I said. She insisted, "I don't care what it is, I'd like to know what causes it." As gently as I could, I informed her that she had been indulging in the sin of self-pity. I shall never forget the look of startled amazment on her face. I don't think I would have gotten a more spontaneous response had I reached across the table and slapped her face. Fortunately, I recalled enough of our previous conversation to give her an illustration.

She had just told me how disgusted she was with the chairman of the Christian Education Committee. It seems she had formulated a project which she had been burdened about that would greatly help the young people's ministry in the church. She took it to the Missionary Committee because it had to do with future missionary volunteers. They passed it on to the Trustees because it involved finances. The Trustees passed it on to the Deacon Board because it involved the spiritual life of the church. Then it was discussed by the entire Advisory Board, composed of every elected officer in the congregation, and finally it received the unanimous vote of the church. Everyone was in a joyous mood; they had a good time of prayer anticipating God's use of this program in the future to salvage many of their youthful volunteers for the mission field.

Then it happened! The Chairman of the Board of Christian Education came to her and critically asserted, "I'd like to know why you and your husband always bypass the Board of Christian Education! It's obvious you don't feel that our Board is a necessary part of this church. I think I'll resign." For the first time the pastor's wife realized that she had inadvertently bypassed this particular board. From this point I took a chance and began to surmise her thought-pattern by saying, "You no doubt came home from prayer meeting that night and indulged in such thoughts as, 'Who does he think he is, criticizing me for a project that received the unanimous vote of the church? I'm the one who is going to do most of the work. It's adding a lot of burdens to my already heavy schedule, and what thanks do I get for it? This man is more concerned about his own petty approval than he is in the ongoing of the Lord's work.' The next day you indulged in similar self-pitying thoughts so that today you are reaping the harvest of self-pity; just as sunshine follows rain, depression follows self-pity." Dr. Maxwell Maltz made the statement, "No one can deny that there is also a perverse sense of satisfaction in feeling sorry for yourself."[6] The Bible tells us, "Whatsoever a man soweth, that shall he also reap." Whenever a person sows the seeds of self-pity, he reaps the results of self-pity in depression.

One of the best cases of self-diagnosis on this matter appeared in the sports page of the *San Diego Union*. One of the best-known football coaches in the National Football League, a former all-pro quarterback of tremendous ability, electrified the sports world by resigning suddenly. He had a good team and a brilliant quarterback, and he expected to win the National Football League championship. Somehow things seemed to go against him, and although the team won the hard games, they seemed to lose some of the easy ones. Immediately after his resignation he went into seclusion, and only after entreaties by the owners of the team, plus the other players and coaches, was he induced to reconsider, which he finally did. Later, when interviewed by sympathetic reporters, he said of the matter, "The thing that I thought of last—not quitting—was the thing I should have thought of first. I have lived a life of not being a quitter, but that's exactly what I was doing— quitting. I wasn't being rational. I don't know what happened. I just wasn't thinking right." When asked when he made the decision to return to the football team, he replied, "*When I quit feeling sorry for myself and came to my senses.* That's why I'm called the Dutchman; I guess I have to learn the hard way."

Happy is the man who, like this great football coach, can face the weakness of self-pity and diagnose it as the cause for depression. That is half the battle. For once we understand that self-pity produces depression, and that it is a sin, all we have to do is go to God for His cure. The cure for self-pity is identically the same as the cure for fear and anger, or any other human weakness, and will be dealt with in detail in the next chapter.

REFERENCES

1. Cramer, op. cit., page 35.
2. McMillen, op. cit., page 111.
3. D. Martyn Lloyd-Jones, *Spiritual Depression—Its Causes and Cure,* ® Pickering and Inglis Ltd., page 17.
4. McMillen, op. cit., page 65.
5. Ibid., page 110.
6. Maltz, op. cit., page 148.

CHAPTER 11

How To Overcome Your Weaknesses

Using The Temperaments to Good Advantage

The basic purpose in giving this temperament study is that we might examine both our strengths and weaknesses and go to the Holy Spirit for His filling and have His strength for our weaknesses. Dr. Henry Brandt has defined a mature person as one who "is sufficiently objective about himself to have examined both his strengths and his weaknesses and has a planned program for overcoming his weaknesses." With the aid of this temperament study you can examine both your strengths and weaknesses and, we trust, be able to construct a planned program for overcoming your weaknesses.

By closely examining the four temperament classifications, and by objectively looking at yourself, you should readily be able to determine which type you are. Keep in mind that no one is a single temperament type. Most people are predominantly one type with tendencies of at least one of the others. Once you have determined your basic temperament, pay close attention to your strengths and weaknesses. It is not God's will that your natural traits be destroyed. It is His will that Christ be glorified in every area of your life within the framework of your own personality. You may find that some of the natural strengths are being neglected in your life, or that others are being over-used until your actions are "the work of the flesh."

An honest examination of your weaknesses can be most helpful in pointing out the areas of your life that need the anointing of the Holy Spirit. Remember one important fact: If you are a Christian, you do not have to be a slave to your natural weaknesses! "Now thanks be unto God, which always causeth us to triumph in Christ . . ." (II Corinthians 2:14).

God in His wise providence has created each of us for "His pleasure" (Revelation 4:11); therefore, no man should despise his temperament, but recognize that we are "fearfully and wonderfully made" and that God utilizes man's natural temperament when it is filled with His Spirit. God has made each of us for a specific purpose; by God's power we will become the finished vessels God wants to use.

Using the temperament studies, determine which temperament you are, make a list of your natural weaknesses, and then seek the filling of the Holy Spirit to overcome them.

After hearing a series of messages on Spirit-controlled temperament, a Christian salesman gave himself some careful

X-RAY OF MY TEMPERAMENT

	SANGUINE	CHOLERIC	MELANCHOLY	PHLEGMATIC
STRONG TENDENCIES	Enjoying Optimistic Friendly	Not discouraged easily Optimistic Leader Team player Decisive Adventurous	Faithful friend Self-sacrificing	Good under pressure Witty Dependable Enjoys humor
WEAKNESSES	Restless Weak-willed Great starter Slow finisher Actions based upon feelings	Impetuous Lack of compassion Hard Impatient	Critical Moody	Tease Indifferent Lazy
SPIRITUAL WEAKNESSES	Lust Lack of direction	Impatience	Critical	
NEGATIVE RESULTS OF THE ABOVE TENDENCIES	Financial problems Easy to over-extend time Unable to stay at one task for a period of time Wastes time in talking Starts many programs Procrastination Easily distracted Impatient with melancholies Place time emphasis in wrong areas Poor study habits Nervous as to sounds, etc. Instant reaction to immediate circumstances	Rash decisions Overly strict with children Set too high standards Easy to take credit for what God has done Lack of kindness Always prompt Argumentative	Will take time from business to run errands Take dislike to people who get in my way or have different views Expect too much from the children Meddler	Hurt people with unkind jest Do not put out full effort at a consistent pace

scrutiny and came up with the preceding chart showing his conclusions. I am not endorsing his method of analysis, but feel that it showed such thorough self-examination that it bears reproducing. He may not have diagnosed correctly the degrees of his temperament, for he considered himself about 45 percent sanguine, 35 percent choleric, 10 percent melancholy and 10 percent phlegmatic. Actually, he was probably a pleasant combination of sanguine-choleric. If you plan to use this form of analysis, I would suggest an additional category—that of "needed strengths."

Selfishness—The Cause of Man's Weaknesses

The following chart more simply identifies the natural weaknesses of each temperament.

As already pointed out, the sanguine-choleric temperaments

Extrovert   **Introvert**

Sanguine	Choleric	Melancholic	Phlegmatic
Weak-willed	Self-sufficient	Moody	Indolent
Restless	Impetuous	Self-centered	Teasing
Egotistical	Cruel	Critical	Stubborn
Emotionally unstable	Hot-tempered	Pessimistic	Indecisive

Anger   Fear

Selfishness

are extrovertish and have a predominant anger problem, while the melancholy and phlegmatic temperaments tend to be introvertish and have a predominant fear problem. The chart clearly shows how these two, and for that matter all of man's basic weaknesses, stem from selfishness. Man's self-interest is what causes him to be restless, weak-willed, hot-tempered, impetuous, self-centered, lazy, critical, fearful or depressed. Selfishness was the original sin of Satan (Isaiah 14), Adam and Eve (Genesis 3), and Cain. A study of human history will reveal man's inhumanity to man caused by selfishness. It is man's selfishness which is the basic cause of all the heartache and misery from the beginning of time to the twentieth century. Egotism, self-centeredness, self-contemplation, self-consciousness and many other words are used to describe it, but they do not limit the fact that man's basic weakness is selfishness. This is not only true of man in his relationship to God, but in his relationship to his fellowman.

When the Ten Commandments are the standard, you will find that the unselfish man will keep them whereas the selfish man will break them. For example, the man who is unselfish toward God will humbly obey God and worship Him only; he will not take His name in vain nor will he take unto himself any graven images; and he will keep the Lord's Day rather than desecrate it for selfish purposes. In relationship to his fellowmen, the unselfish man will honor his father and mother; he will not steal, nor will he be so inconsiderate of his neighbor as to bear false witness against him, commit adultery with his wife, or covet that which is his neighbor's. From this it can easily be seen that the selfish heart is the root of all sin. It may take a variety of forms, but evil can still be traced to selfishness.

One of the hardest things for man to learn is the Lord Jesus' principle, "He that findeth his life shall lose it: and he that loseth his life for My sake shall find it" (Matthew 10:39). When man's faith and consecration have reached the point that he is willing to give his life completely to Jesus Christ, the Spirit of God will cure his problem of selfishness. This cure is basic, but through force of habit there will be occasional reversals to previous patterned behavior; when he does not continue to "abide in Christ" or "walk in the Spirit," he will revert to former behavior.

The Holy Spirit—God's Cure
For Temperament Weaknesses

As pointed out in chapter 6, the nine characteristics of the Spirit-filled man supply a strength for every one of your natural weaknesses. It is not God's will that you be dominated by your inherited weaknesses, but that you be filled with the Holy Spirit and thus freed from them.

The Holy Spirit does not automatically indwell every human being. On the contrary, He indwells only those who have received Jesus Christ by faith as Savior from sin. The Bible tells us, "If any man have not the Spirit of Christ, he is none of His" (Romans 8:9). That is, he is not a child of God if he does not have the Holy Spirit. But if he trusts in Christ, then God has sent the Holy Spirit into his heart. If you have never received Jesus Christ as your Lord and Savior, then your primary need is to right now humble yourself and invite Him into your life. The Bible tells us, "Whosoever shall call upon the name of the Lord shall be saved" (Romans 10:13). If you are willing to acknowledge Jesus Christ as Lord of your life, then invite Him in or, as the Bible says, "Call upon the name of the Lord." Salvation is not a long, tedious process—it is an instantaneous experience. Jesus called it being "born again" and likened it to physical birth. Your physical birth was an instantaneous experience, and by the same token so should be your spiritual birth. It is true that the Spirit of God speaks to our hearts through the Word of God over a long period of time, and many people go through a long process of considering their acceptance of Christ, but in order to receive Him one must have a distinct experience of calling upon the name of the Lord.

Jesus Christ Himself said to individuals, "Behold, I stand at the door, and knock: if any man hear My voice, and open the door, I will come in to him, and will sup with him, and he with Me" (Revelation 3:20). The word "sup" means to fellowship; if you desire the fellowship of Christ through His Spirit, then you must invite Him into your life. Only by this means can you have your past sins forgiven, your soul saved, and your life indwelt by the Holy Spirit. The Holy Spirit fills the lives only of believers, and believers are those who have invited Jesus Christ to come in and dwell within them as Lord and Savior. If you are seeking any other way of overcoming your weaknesses, or for fellowshiping with God, you will seek in vain. Jesus Christ said, "I am the way, the truth, and the life: no man cometh unto the Father, but by Me" (John 14:6). If you have never called upon the name of the Lord Jesus, may I urge you right now to do so. He is the only way to the Father, the only source of power to overcome your weaknesses.

Overcoming Your Weaknesses

If you are a Christian, you already possess the power to overcome your weaknesses! That power is the Holy Spirit. If you are filled with the Holy Spirit as defined in chapters 6 and 7, He will overcome your weaknesses. If, however, you find that you grieve or quench the Holy Spirit by indulging in anger, fear, or any of the other weaknesses on the preceding weakness chart, there is a cure for you. In spite of its general nature, you will find the following planned program for overcoming your weaknesses to be very effective.

1. Face your weaknesses as sin!

Don't offer excuses for your weaknesses such as "that's my nature" or "I can't help it, that's the way I am." Too many Christians are mental escape artists and refuse to face their shortcomings and weaknesses as sin. Just because escapism is a common practice of our day, there is no excuse for Christians to indulge in it. Be a realist. If you know Christ, you can face anything. The Bible tells us, "I can do all things through Christ which strengtheneth me" (Philippians 4:13). Either that statement is true or false. If it is false, then God is a liar, the Bible is untrustworthy, and we can forget the entire Christian message! This position is unthinkable and, frankly, would leave man with no possible cure. If a man does not know Jesus Christ, he may refuse to face the facts of his own weaknesses, for he does not have access to the power of God's Spirit to cure them. But that is not your problem if you are a Christian. Therefore, face your weaknesses as sin.

Alcoholics Anonymous makes it very clear that the first step toward curing alcoholism is for an alcoholic to face the fact that he is an alcoholic. By the same token, if you do not face the fact that you are an angry, bitter, resentful Christian or a fearful, anxious, worried Christian, you will go to your grave dominated by anger or fear. If you are a depressive individual as a result of indulging in the sin of self-pity, you will go to your grave marred by the effects of long periods of depression. No matter what your weakness, take the first giant step toward the cure by facing the fact that it is a sin and then go to God for His marvelous cure.

2. Confess your sin every time!

I John 1:9 tells us, "If we confess our sins, He is faithful and just to forgive us our sins, and to cleanse us from all unrighteousness." Every Christian should memorize that verse and use it every time he sins. That verse, although used appropriately for sinners needing salvation, is really written to Christians. John addresses "my little children," for he is speaking to those who are children of God by faith. Someone has called this verse "the Christian's bar of soap." It is intended to be used regularly to keep us from going through long periods of time with sin in our lives.

The Bible tells us: "If I regard iniquity in my heart, the Lord will not hear me" (Psalm 66:18). A Christian's prayer life is short-circuited as long as there is unconfessed sin in his life. If he does not face his anger and fear as sin, his prayer effectiveness will be curtailed. However, that prayer life can be reestablished the moment confession is sought.

"How often should I use I John 1:9?" is a question that has often been directed to me. My answer is always the same: "Every time you sin and as soon as you are conscious of the sin." Don't let time elapse between the sin and the confession. Every time you "blow your top" or become fearful or depressed, you grieve or quench the Holy Spirit. The instant you are conscious of that sin, confess it and thank God for His faithful forgiveness and restoration.

3. Ask your loving heavenly Father to take away this habit
"And this is the confidence that we have in Him, that if we ask anything according to His will, He

heareth us: And if we know that He hear us, what-
soever we ask, we know that we have the petitions
that we desired of Him." (I John 5:14-15)

Victory over fear and anger is the will of God. These verses make it crystal clear that we can be confident in having the answer to our prayers when we ask according to His will. Therefore, when we ask God to cure our habitual weaknesses, we can be confident He will. Jesus said, "All power is given unto Me in heaven and in earth. Go ye therefore and teach all nations . . ." (Matthew 28:18-19). Since the Lord Jesus has all power and has demonstrated that power by creating the heavens and the earth, which includes man, certainly He has the power to overcome our natural weaknesses.

4. Believe God has given the victory

Romans 14:23 tells us that "whatsoever is not of faith is sin." Many Christians are hindered right here because they do not "feel cured" after they have asked for the cure. Our feeling has nothing to do with it. Instead, we need to rely upon the promises of God and expect victory. You can do all things through Christ which strengthens you. That includes being gracious instead of angry, trusting instead of fearful. Commit your way unto the Lord instead of worrying about things.

The best way I know to accept victory—after you meet the conditions—is to thank Him by faith for that victory. I Thessalonians 5:18 tells us, "In everything give thanks: for this is the will of God in Christ Jesus concerning you." Since the will of God is that we give thanks in everything, then by faith we can give thanks for the cure for our weaknesses when we have obediently asked Him for victory.

5. Ask for the filling of the Holy Spirit (Luke 11:13)

To further help you to overcome your weaknesses, I would remind you to ask for the filling of the Holy Spirit as outlined in chapter 7. If you have already faced your weaknesses as sin, confessed them, and asked the heavenly Father by faith for victory, then why not prepare your life for service by asking for His filling, again believing that God does what you ask?

6. Walk in the Spirit and abide in Christ (Galatians 5:16; John 15:1-11).

The Lord Jesus said, "If ye abide in Me and My words abide in you, ye shall ask what ye will and it shall be done unto you." The "abiding life" is the "Spirit-filled life." Both are the way the Lord Jesus wants us to live in this generation. The following steps are suggested as a method of walking in the Spirit or abiding in Christ:

Be filled with the Holy Spirit as shown above.

Allow the Word of God to have a regular part of your life. Since the Word is a supernatural Book, it accomplishes a supernatural work in the life of the believer who reads it. A Spirit-filled Christian will read the Word of God since it is his only source of spiritual food. To be faithful in this regard, one should set aside a regular time for reading. If you are a new Christian, may I suggest that you start with the Gospel of John; read I John, Philippians and Ephesians several times; and then read the entire New Testament. Until a Christian has read through the New Testament, he should not turn to the Old Testament. Although regular reading habits are essential for long-range walking in the Spirit, avoid the danger of becoming legalistic about your daily devotions. Certainly the Lord understands when you go to bed at 2 a.m. and have to get up at 6 a.m. and rush out to an early appointment. He who loved us enough to die for us understands the need of our body for rest. He also understands the wild pace we live. Therefore, we can still enjoy the filling of the Holy Spirit whether we have read the Word on a given day or not. But a Spirit-filled Christian will desire to feed his soul on the Word of God whenever possible.

Daily practice of prayer. Because prayer is communion with God, it should also have a regular place in the life of the Christian who is walking in the Spirit. When we speak of prayer, most people think of protracted periods in the solitude of their room. These protracted times of prayer are beneficial and should have a regular part in a Christian's life, but that is not all there is to prayer. The Bible tells us, "Men ought always to pray and not to faint" (Luke 18:1) and that we should "pray without ceasing" (I Thessalonians 5:17). The Christian walking in the Spirit will live a life of prayer. He will commune with Christ through the Spirit about everything in his life. He will ask His instruction about work and his family decisions—in effect, he will follow the admonition, "In all thy ways acknowledge Him." (Proverbs 3:6)

Continually yield yourself to the Holy Spirit. Romans 6:11-13 tells us to "yield ye your members as instruments of righteousness unto God." The abiding Christian, or the Christian walking in the Spirit, is one who continually yields himself to God. That is, every plan and activity of life is conditioned on the premise, "Thy will be done." There is nothing wrong with a Christian having a desire in a particular direction, provided it does not violate the principles of the Word of God, but the desire should always be patterned after our Lord's prayer in Gethsemane: "Not my will but Thine be done." It is only when we willfully, stubbornly demand our way that we are on dangerous ground.

As a college student, if you desire to change colleges this year or desire to invite a friend home for the holidays, you don't have to fear disobeying the Lord. Our desires can very well be of God. Always remember that God is interested in giving "good things to them that ask Him" (Matthew 7:11). But the yielded Christian walking in the Spirit will condition every desire on the basis, "If the Lord will . . ." I would like to do this or that.

Serve Christ. The Lord Jesus said, "If any man serve Me, him will My Father honor" (John 12:26). He also said to His disciples, "Follow Me, and I will make you fishers of men" (Matthew 4:19), and "If any man will come after Me, let him deny himself, and take up his cross daily, and follow Me" (Luke 9:23). Jesus Christ wants us to follow Him in Christian service. All Christians are saved to serve Him. You are either serving Him or being served. As someone has said, every Christian is either a missionary force or a mission field. God uses men to do His work, and God seeks to fill your life by not only overcoming your weaknesses, but making you productive and effective in His service. This productivity is not only eternally meaningful, but it is actually therapeutic.

Man is so devised that he is frustrated when he does not serve his Creator. The happiest people in the world are those who are productive for Jesus Christ. A school teacher friend who is predominantly of the melancholy temperament and has experienced protracted periods of depression recently told me that he had one bright day during a lengthy depressed state. It was the result of a chance opportunity to witness of his personal faith in Jesus Christ to another school teacher. He enthusiastically stated, "That was the best feeling I had all week." If that dear brother had been walking in the Spirit and desiring to be available to communicate his testimony to the hundreds of other souls with whom he came in contact, he would not have had any periods of depression.

When you get right down to it, the depressed individual comes to the decision: Am I going to yield myself to Christ to serve Him, or am I going to indulge in the sin of self-pity? In short, then, the question involves self-pity or service. Your answer to that question under the filling and leading of the Holy Spirit determines your contentment of heart in this life and reward in the life to come.

Walking in the Spirit is a way of life. Admittedly, it is a supernatural way of life, but it is the result of the indwelling of God's Holy Spirit, who is supernatural. It is nothing short of what we can expect as a result of our receiving Christ, for the Word of God promises that old things pass away and "all things have become new" (II Corinthians 5:17).

The Power of Habit

Habit can be a vicious force that dominates many people. Do not be surprised if you find that you revert to the habit of giving in to your weakness, whether it be anger, fear, depression, or any of their derivatives. Just remember, you do not have to be dominated by that habit (Philippians 4:13). True, the devil will fight you every inch of the way, but just remember, "Greater is He that is in you, than he that is in the world" (I John 4:4). Frequently I find Christians who will try this procedure of facing their weaknesses as sin, confessing them, asking for victory, believing they have the victory, requesting the filling of the Holy Spirit, and walking in that Spirit, only to find that they revert to habit. Too often they give up because of their revision to old habit. This is a trick of the devil! A very simple cure is by faith to repeat these five steps for overcoming your weaknesses every time you sin as soon as you are conscious you have sinned, and eventually you will find that the old habits no longer dominate you.

A man once came to me who was dominated by the sin of blasphemy. As a new Christian he knew that he could no longer use the name of the Lord Jesus Christ in vain. It grieved him, and yet by force of habit he did it without thinking. In a state of deep anguish he cried out, "What can I do to overcome this awful habit?" My answer was, "Every time you use the Lord Jesus' name in vain, face the fact that it's a sin, confess it, ask your heavenly Father to remove the habit, thank Him by faith for His anticipated victory, ask for the filling of the Holy Spirit, and walk in the Spirit." Within three weeks that man came in to tell me joyfully that profanity was a thing of the past. Should the vicious habit of grieving the Spirit through anger or quenching the Holy Spirit through fear or depression be any different? Let me share with you some stories of Christians I know whom God has cured of their weaknesses.

Case Histories of Cured Weaknesses

A young mechanic came into my office one day and told me that he had spent $250 seeing a psychiatrist and that he finally learned his problem: "I hate my mother!" This young man, after six visits to the psychiatrist, was told that because his mother had hopelessly confused his life through alcoholism and sought to turn him and his father against each other, he subconsciously hated her.

As a Christian of about four years, he had been married for a year and a half and was very happily adjusting to this new way of life when suddenly his mother was released from an institution for alcoholics. She had no sooner called him on the phone than he and his wife started having problems. He had trouble with men at work. Everything was going wrong, and suddenly he began to develop an ulcer. All he needed to ruin his day was for mother to call him or drop by his garage. He told me that the hair on his arms stood straight up when his mother was within one hundred feet of him. I asked, "If you have been seeing a psychiatrist all this time, why have you

.

come to me?" His answer was rather interesting. "The psychiatrist told me what's wrong, but he didn't tell me how to cure it." (About the only cure that I have seen from the school of psychiatry for intense anger came to my attention recently. A psychiatrist advised that a person should "find out what it is that annoys you and avoid it." I instantly wondered what a man does when he finds out that it's his wife that annoys him. Of course, that could be one of the contributing factors to the high divorce rate in America.)

In a sense, psychiatry has no answer because it has no supernatural source to change the angry disposition of man. Thank God, this young man knew Jesus Christ and by applying the above formula could not only come into the presence of his mother with his hair lying flat on his arms, but could talk to her kindly and graciously without grieving the Holy Spirit.

Another young man was referred to me for the counseling of his wife, who had been seeing a psychiatrist twice a week. Since neither of them came to our church, I couldn't understand how he expected me to get her to see me, so during our telephone conversation I suggested, "Why don't you come by and see me first? Then you can go home and tell your wife that you have counseled with a minister and suggest that she come in and see me also." He thought that was a good idea and made an appointment for the following Monday during his lunch hour.

I shall never forget that as he came through the door the noon siren blew, as was the custom every Monday in San Diego. He looked at his watch and very proudly announced, "I've kept my record intact. I've never been late for an appointment in my life!" As soon as he was seated, he went into an angry, 25-minute description of all the misery his wife had caused him and how psychotic she was. When he had finally unburdened himself, I began to present to him the gospel of Jesus Christ in the form of the Four Spiritual Laws which my 16-year-old daughter had introduced to me as the result of her training at a Campus Crusade for Christ conference. Because I had noticed that the Holy Spirit had used this method of presenting Christ in the lives of others, I wanted to try it.

The young engineer quickly informed me, "Well, I don't believe in Christ; it's not that I'm an atheist, I just don't believe." Squelching for the first time my ministerial inclination to present the wonderful claims of Christ and the abundant proofs for His personal deity, I ignored his statement and went right on presenting the Four Spiritual Laws. When I finished, after drawing the two circles showing the nonchristian and the Christian life, I asked, "Which of these two circles represents your life?" I was rather surprised when he replied, pointing to the nonchristian circle, "Oh, that represents my life. That's a picture of me, right there." Then rather hesitantly, because he claimed not to believe in Christ, I said, "Well, do you know of any reason why right now you couldn't invite Jesus Christ into your life?" To my utter amazement, he looked me straight in the face and said, "No, in fact, that is exactly what I need." With that he got down on his knees and began to pray. He first confessed what an angry, bitter, resentful, revengeful young man he was, and he asked Jesus Christ to forgive him and come into his life. When he finished, he sat down and began to weep. I watched him for several minutes, after which he sighed and said, "I've never felt so relaxed in all my life!" Then it was that I saw the evidence of the working of God's Spirit in his life as a new Christian, for he said, "By the way, Pastor, all those things I told you about my wife aren't really true. Forget it. Most of the problem has been me."

Two weeks later when he returned, I was intrigued by the fact that he had memorized the verses assigned him, completed a Bible study, and read his Bible every day simply because he was that kind of methodical individual. When I asked him, "How is your wife?" he again revealed the complete transformation miraculously accomplished in his life by the Holy Spirit when he said, "She's not doing too good, but I guess that's understandable. It's going to take a long time to overcome the effects of all the things that I have done to her in our married life." This loving, compassionate, gracious young man was nothing like the angry, vitriolic, bitter individual of two weeks before—another evidence of the power of the Holy Spirit to overcome man's natural weaknesses.

An interesting result of this experience appeared two months later. His wife, inspired by the transformation in her husband's life, got down on her knees in their home and invited the Lord Jesus Christ into her life. She has been delivered of her problems of fear and no longer sees a psychiatrist.

An often-depressed and fear-dominated housewife came to see me. In the course of counseling she revealed what a miserable life she lived. She had gone through shock treatments five years before and sensed herself going back into that same cycle of fear and depression that she so dreaded. She was raised in a Christian home and was married to a fine Christian businessman, but she still was dominated by her weakness of fear. One of her problems involved a particular sin committed 11 years before which she could not get out of her mind. Though she could say, "I know God has forgiven me," she would add, "But I can't forgive myself."

However, I was suspicious that she really didn't understand the extent of God's forgiveness, so I assigned her the project of doing a research study on all the biblical teaching on God's forgiveness of sin. Two weeks later she was radiant when she returned. For the first time in her life she knew what it was to have peace with God about her old sin. Gradually that sin became a thing of the past in her mind, and many of her fears vanished. Yet additional counseling was necessary because she still had long periods of depression.

One day I was able to confront her with the fact that her depression was the result of self-pity, and that just as God had cured her of her fears of the past when she recognized His forgiveness, so He could cure her of the depressed periods if she would just quit feeling sorry for herself. Being perfectionist-prone, she indulged in mental "chewing" to herself about her husband's careless habits around the house. She would often grumble to herself because he was not more expressive of his love. In fact, she acknowledged there were many areas in her life where she felt sorry for herself. When confronted with the sin involved in this deadly habit, she confessed it as a sin and went away armed with the above method for overcoming her weaknesses. It was only a few weeks before she called to tell me that she no longer needed to come in for counseling. I have received several notes of appreciation from her, and her husband thanks me regularly when we meet for "the transformation in my wife." It wasn't the counseling; it was the Holy Spirit who overcame her weakness.

These are only a few of the case histories that could be offered to illustrate the fact that God can overcome your weaknesses. We all have a tendency to exaggerate our problems, and if it is any comfort to you, remember, "There hath no temptation taken you but such as is common to man: but God is faithful, who will not suffer you to be tempted above that ye are able; but will with the temptation also make a way to escape, that ye may be able to bear it" (I Corinthians 10:13).

Whatever your weaknesses, they are "common to man" because they are a result of your temperament, your background, your training and motivation. If you have received Jesus Christ as your Savior and Lord, the Holy Spirit is now your motivation and the most important part of your character. The abundant life that Jesus Christ came to give you (John 10:10b) is yours through the filling of the Holy Spirit. If you have been dominated by your weaknesses, take heart. Jesus Christ can overcome them! A whole new way of life is now open to you as you let the Holy Spirit control your temperament.

CHAPTER 12

Spirit-Modified Temperaments

When the Holy Spirit comes into a man's life, he begins immediately to modify the human temperament. As a counselor, I have had the great joy of observing the unmistakable work of the Spirit on the natural temperament of a person until it is almost impossible to see traces of the original temperament. It is particularly encouraging to observe this change when the person does not know a thing about temperament; he is just changed by the Holy Spirit.

This temperament modification is to be expected. Being "born again" is a supernatural experience and as such should have a supernatural effect upon an individual. The degree of modification in a person's temperament will be in direct proportion to the filling of his life with the Holy Spirit. The Holy Spirit will automatically introduce new traits and characteristics into an individual's nature.

The nine characteristics of the Holy Spirit as seen in Galatians 5:22-23 provide a working basis to show what God can do with the raw material of our temperament. We shall again examine each temperament and show how the Holy Spirit supplies strength for each of our natural weaknesses. This change will take place gradually and usually subconsciously.

The Spirit-Filled Sanguine

Mr. Sanguine will always be an extrovert—even after he is filled with the Holy Spirit. He will also be an energetic, infectious and compassionate soul. Because he is so talkative his conversation will be one of the first apparent changes in his life. He will probably talk just as much, but it will be far different. He will learn a new vocabulary, dropping the often used profane and dirty words that are so natural to the unsaved Sanguine. He will still tell jokes as he enlivens social gatherings, but now he will enjoy wholesome humor rather than smutty or suggestive stories. He will still feel the emotions of others but with purposeful compassion. Instead of just weeping with those that weep he will now encourage them by sharing the promises of God and pointing them to Jesus, the author and finisher of our faith.

Mr. Sanguine's weakness of will is probably his most serious problem. When filled with the Holy Spirit he will find a new strength of character that keeps him from "going along with the boys," or "following the path of least resistance." He will become more consistent in his personal life, even to the point

SELF-CONTROL

that he becomes more organized and dependable. He will learn to say "no" to some opportunities in preference to doing a good job with the responsibilities he already has. Though he is naturally receptive to his surroundings he will avoid being alone with pretty secretaries or flirting with other women. His sense of values begins to change and his own wife begins to look more attractive to him and the happiness of his family will seem more important.

This dynamic man will find a challenging new purpose in life, to be used of God. Once he has tasted the joy of seeing the Holy Spirit use his life to draw other men to the Savior, the old way of life seems very insignificant.

A salesman friend of mine took me to lunch one day and shared his problems, revealing himself as almost pure Sanguine. One quarter he led the office in sales and then he went into an apathetic period when he sold nothing. He had a problem with lust, and his past devil-may-care life was becoming attractive again. He gave up his Sunday School class and found petty excuses to skip some church services. He was thoroughly miserable!

I pointed out that the Holy Spirit was not about to let him

go, for "whom the Lord loveth, he chasteneth" and his misery was of the Lord. We then discussed the Spirit-filled life, and it made sense to him. Gradually I watched this man become in practice what he was in the Spirit. A new self-control came into his life; he has been first or second in sales each month for over a year now; his family life is transformed. But even better, God has used him mightily in the lives of many business men, both churched and unchurched. Believe me, he is not about to trade his Spirit-filled experience for the old Sanguine life.

Another strength the Holy Spirit supplies Mr. Sanguine is peace. He is restless by nature but as the Spirit brings a new purpose into his life he also produces a relaxed peace. He will

PEACE

learn to commit his way unto the Lord, and instead of engendering strife and confusion he will have a more pleasing, soothing effect on people. This will help him avoid many unpleasant situations brought on by his own rash judgments.

His newfound peace and self-control will help control his fiery temper. By applying the formula for overcoming his weakness of anger as given in the preceding chapter, he will avoid excessive outbursts that often prove embarrassing and humiliating. Thus he will have many periods of peace where previously he had gone through the tortures of shame, repentance and hostility from others.

HUMILITY

Since Mr. Sanguine is inclined to be egocentric by nature, the Holy Spirit will introduce a new humility into his life. He will gradually become concerned for the needs and feelings of others. He will not ridicule some poor soul in public to get a laugh out of the group, but will be considerate of another's feelings and seek his humor elsewhere. His conversation will no longer revolve around himself, but around the Lord Jesus Christ and Christian work. In short, his egotism will give place to a meekness foreign to his nature, and he will cease to be the braggadocio character of the past.

This new humility will make new friends for him and since he is such an expressive person his faith will be contagious.

The Apostle Peter is a good example of the Spirit-filled Sanguine. After the day of Pentecost Peter used his lips to preach Jesus Christ in power. There was an apparent consistency and control in Peter's life from that point on, and absolutely no self-seeking tendencies. He was still a leader, but his conduct before the Sanhedrin in Acts 4 shows a Spirit-dominated restraint foreign to his nature. His life was used greatly to glorify Christ because he was Spirit-filled.

Many a Sanguine Christian has been used of God to share his faith as he has sought the filling of the Holy Spirit and walked in the Spirit. Great will be their reward in heaven! Sad to say, many a Sanguine Christian has gone restlessly and unproductively through life, stirring up strife, hurting other believers and actually hindering the work of their church. They will be saved, "so as by fire" (I Cor. 3:15), but have little or no reward—all because they did not heed God's command to "be filled with the Holy Spirit." (Eph. 5:18)

The Spirit-Filled Choleric

The Spirit-filled Choleric will invariably produce a dynamic and effective Christian leader. His strong will power, directed by the Holy Spirit toward eternal goals, makes him very productive. He will "go the extra mile" in getting the Lord's work done. In fact, many of the great leaders in church history possessed a heavy dose of Choleric temperament. His natural productivity is not because he has superior intelligence but is the result of his active mind and dogged determination.

A sales company years ago determined that the difference between the very successful salesman and the ordinary salesman was 17 percent greater effort. The Choleric Christian is most apt to go that extra 17 percent, and when his natural optimism is added you find a man who is willing to "attempt great things for God."

The leadership of the Choleric has proven a danger in Christian history when the Choleric gave in to the temptation to take credit for what God has done with his life, grieving the Spirit and reverting back to doing the work of the Lord in his own energy. Because of his natural abilities, it takes some time for his neglect of the Spirit to become apparent to others and they continue to follow him. Paul said, "Be ye followers of me, even as I also am of Christ." (I Cor. 11:1) We should follow Christian leaders only as they follow Christ, as he has revealed himself in his will in the Word of God.

In spite of the above mentioned good qualities of Mr. Choleric, it should be pointed out that he has the temperament with the greatest spiritual needs, but is often unaware of that fact. Frequently he is unwilling to acknowledge it even when made aware of it. He is often content to do "the work of the Lord" independent of the Holy Spirit. Happy is the Choleric (and his family) who recognizes with Paul that he must "die daily" and is willing to say, "I am crucified with Christ, nevertheless I live, yet not I but Christ liveth in me." (Gal. 2:20)

Among the first changes in the Spirit-filled Choleric will be his love for people. He will gradually look at people as individuals for whom Christ died, and a genuine compassion for others will characterize his outlook. If properly taught, he will see the need of sending missionaries to the pagan countries of the world.

LOVE

One nonchristian, upon hearing that his cousin was going to become a Bible translator and "bury his life in the jungles of Brazil," made the following statement: "I know what I would do—I'd take a machine gun and mow those natives down!" During the missionary's first term on the field, the cousin was converted. The Holy Spirit transformed him so that he met his missionary cousin at the plane when he returned after four years and outfitted the whole family with new clothes. Recently the convert told me that he and his wife are going to work for Wycliffe Bible Translators to raise money and find workers to get the gospel to the Bibleless tribes of the world! Only the Holy Spirit could put love in a heart like that!

The Spirit-filled Choleric is going to experience an enriching peace that is not limited to periods of activity. He will gradually

PEACE

find it easier to "wait on the Lord" for his wisdom rather than rushing off half-cocked on the basis of his intuitive judgment. As the peace of God replaces his innate anger he finds that he is happier and more contented. Instead of "stewing" and "churning" over some injustice done him, he learns to "cast all his care" on the Lord. If vengeance is to be taken he lets the Lord do it. In short, he comes to value the uninterrupted walk with Christ through the filling of the Holy Spirit.

In addition to gaining spiritual and emotional peace, he avoids the ulcers that he would otherwise have. In one family of four Cholerics I know, the strongest Choleric is the only one who does not have ulcers. It is no coincidence that he is the only one of the four told about the Spirit-filled life.

GENTLENESS

GOODNESS

The other four spiritual characteristics so sorely needed by Mr. Choleric are gentleness, goodness, long-suffering and meekness. To make best use of his life and to enrich him, the Holy Spirit wants to create these characteristics in him.

When filled with the Spirit, Mr. Choleric will turn from his tendency to be brusque, crude and sometimes obnoxious and be polite, gracious and courteous. Instead of ignoring his wife in public he will begin to treat her respectfully. Not because consideration and courtesy are meaningful to him, but because it is meaningful to her, and is a good testimony to Christ. It would be inconceivable to imagine the Lord Jesus walking through a door in front of a lady and letting it swing back into her face. Neither will it be a practice of his Spirit-filled servant.

131

LONGSUFFERING

MEEKNESS

When the Holy Spirit introduces a refreshing meekness and humility to the proud attitude of Mr. Choleric, he will have a natural desire to do things for others and will find a new patience in their inconsistencies and weaknesses. Instead of feeling a sense of superiority when he is confronted with another's weakness, he may thank God for the gracious gift of self-control. It is a gift which he will treasure increasingly with its use.

Since the world is filled with needy people, Mr. Spirit-filled Choleric will never run out of things to do and people to help. Now, however, instead of wasting time doing those things that satisfy his quest for activity, he will be led of the Spirit to invest himself in sharing the one thing man needs most—a personal knowledge of and experience with Jesus Christ. His newfound graciousness, patience, and tact will make him a productive soul-winner. The result for him will be a rich and rewarding life invested in people for the Lord's sake, and many rewards laid up in heaven in obedience to the Lord's command.

The power of the Spirit to change the Choleric temperament was illustrated to me some years ago. We had a high school boy in our church who was downright mean. Our four-year-old girl would not go near him. During the boy's senior year, the Holy Spirit convicted him deeply, and although he had been baptized and was a member of the church, he realized that he had never really been born again. On New Year's Eve he got down on his knees and invited Jesus Christ to come into his life and become his Lord and Savior.

The change in that boy was amazing! A new gentility and kindness came into his life that was unbelievable. Two months later he was walking on the sidewalk just after church as our little daughter came down the steps from the nursery department. Smiling at her, he held out his arms, and to my utter amazement she leaped into them and gave him a big hug. I was convinced that this was not the same boy—though he looked the same outwardly!

The Spirit-filled Choleric is going to enjoy many blessings unshared by the natural Choleric. Not the least of these is love and companionship. The natural Choleric has few close friends. People respect him, often admire him, but because they are so afraid of him, very few love him. When filled with the Spirit, he will have the kind of gracious personality that draws people to him on a genuine and lasting basis. The natural Choleric, when aware that he is unloved even by his own family, may say, "I could care less." But in his heart he knows better. Mr. Choleric desperately needs the filling of the Holy Spirit.

The Apostle Paul is probably the best illustration of the Spirit-filled Choleric to be found in the Bible. We first see him in Acts 8 "consenting" to the murder of the first Christian martyr, Stephen. In chapter 9 we find him ". . . yet breathing out threatenings and slaughter against the disciples of the Lord."

If ever there was a description of a raw Choleric, this is it. Yet Bible students are thrilled to find this man so dynamically transformed that the very study of his post-conversion conduct has been used by God to lead many to acknowledge the supernatural power of Jesus Christ as the only explanation for his behavior.

The Spirit-Filled Melancholy

The many talents of the Melancholy temperament are enriched and made productive by the filling of the Holy Spirit.

His rich, sensitive nature will be earnestly attuned to the heart-needs of humanity. No one can more realistically hear the pathetic cries of lost humanity like the Melancholy. When filled with the Spirit he will not just hear them, he will be available to God to do something about them. His analytical perfectionism particularly fit him for the much-needed detail work that is so often neglected by his extrovertish brethren. When filled with the Spirit, instead of being neutralized by irritation at others' disgusting carelessness, he will serve the Lord quietly, "counting it all joy" to be a part in the ongoing of the Savior's Kingdom.

The neglected corners of the world are indebted to the Spirit-filled Melancholy's self-sacrificing for their hearing of the gospel. Many a Christian can look back on a faithful, Spirit-filled Melancholy who doggedly kept after him after others had given up. Because of his great capacity to love, he loves others to the Savior, often suffering many abuses in the process.

Few Christians realize as they sing a beautiful hymn in church, read some meaningful poetry, enjoy such music as the *Messiah,* see some great work of art or read some deep truths of God in a book that they are enjoying the results of the Melancholy's talents, modified and energized by the Holy Spirit.

GOODNESS

The self-centered characteristic of the Melancholy that so often dominates his life will give place to meekness and goodness when he is filled with the Holy Spirit. The best therapy in the world for a Melancholy person is to get his eyes off himself and involved with someone else. I don't know how this can be done without Jesus Christ! When the meekness and goodness of the Spirit take over a Melancholy he really sees that he is the "chiefest of sinners" and the recipient of the unlimited mercy of God.

Although he will never be careless in what he does, he begins to realize that the needs of others are so acute that he must offer himself to God to serve them. His perfectionism is not what really does the job—but the working of the Holy Spirit. When the Spirit finally gets through to the Melancholy that God wants his availability, not his perfectionism, he is ready to be used.

In God's hand, "any old bush will do," and as Paul said, "When I am weak then am I strong." As this meekness pervades his life he can truly enjoy other people in spite of their weaknesses, and he is not tempted to criticize them and thus grieve his sensitive conscience.

A Spirit-filled Melancholy enjoys peaceful sleep while the backslidden Melancholy's bed becomes a torture rack as he relives and rehearses the result of his uncontrolled criticism and caustic remarks. The Spirit-filled Melancholy is content to leave the results to God after doing the best he can in music, art or any field. The flesh-dominated Melancholy is never satisfied.

A Melancholy housewife complained to me about her Sanguine husband's inconsistency. Always late, quite undependable, careless with his clothes and always taking on more than he could do well, he reaped a harvest of criticism. Gently I shared with her that in spite of all her husband's weaknesses God was using him far more than her. As a young Christian, he was a dynamic testimony at work and had won several salesmen and customers to Christ. She could do anything better than he, but she had never led anyone to Christ.

Why was this? Not because he was inconsistent, but because he was available. With her, "the time is never right," she "didn't know the right Bible verses," or "maybe I will offend someone" was her response to the Spirit's leading.

But today she is a soul-winner. The reason is that now, instead of making excuses, she prays, "Lord, here are my lips; if you want to use them they are available." She isn't always just sure how the conversation gets started, but regularly the Spirit uses her. Spirit-induced meekness and goodness make any person available to God, and availability leads to fruitfulness.

The seventh characteristic of the Holy Spirit cancels the Melancholy tendency to pessimism. Pessimism is contagious; but faith cures pessimism. As the Spirit has control of a Melancholy believer, things thought impossible are looked at with the power of God in view. Through faith, Moses the Melancholy became a great leader. So today, many a believer confronted with overwhelming obstacles has looked at them by faith and God has given victory. Most Christians, like Israel of old, "limit God through unbelief." In this day God is looking for men of faith (II Chron. 16:9). He is not looking for geniuses and intellectuals, he is looking for available vessels that have faith enough to believe God for achieving the impossible.

Some years ago I broke my brown sun glasses and in looking for new ones discovered that green glasses make everything look better. The grass looks greener, the sky more blue, in fact, all colors become more vivid. Suddenly it dawned on me that when the Holy Spirit fills a believer he puts on the glasses of faith and everything looks better—the impossible becomes possible, the unattainable attainable. Happy is the Spirit-filled man in these dark days, for the glasses of faith make everything look better. God has used all kinds of men, both in Bible days and throughout Christian history. Some were well-trained geniuses like the Apostle Paul; some were untrained, average men like Peter. But all men in every age who were used of God had one thing in common—faith.

JOY

Mr. Melancholy's natural moodiness is no match for the joy and peace of the Holy Spirit. No one can be filled with the Holy Spirit and be depressed at the same time, even Mr. Melancholy. That doesn't mean he won't be depressed. It does mean that when he is depressed and moody he is not filled with the Holy Spirit. If he occupies himself with the filling of the Holy Spirit instead of his circumstances or himself he will not be moody.

PEACE

Joy and peace come to the Christian from two sources: the Word of God and the gift of the Holy Spirit. (Col. 3:15-17; Eph. 5:18-21) I have known moody Christians who never read the Bible for their own spiritual blessings. They would rather sit around and feel sorry for themselves than read the Word of God. Jesus said, "These things have I spoken unto you, that my joy might remain in you, and that your joy might be full." (John 15:11) The Savior also said, "These things I have spoken unto you, that in me ye might have peace. In the world ye shall have tribulation: but be of good cheer; I have overcome the world." (John 16:33)

The joy and peace of the Spirit-filled Melancholy prepare

him emotionally to unlock the depth of riches God has placed within him. Gradually he will discard the old moody habits as the joy and peace of the Holy Spirit fill his life. As one Spirit-filled Melancholy told me, "Since I have been walking in the Spirit I quit looking for happiness and it dawned on me the other day that I am happy!"

The love of God shed abroad in the believer's heart by the Holy Spirit must have an effect upon a Christian. As God's love floods the Melancholy Christian he gradually is less occupied with himself and more occupied with Christ and others. That in itself is good therapy. Under the power of this love, Mr. Melancholy becomes a different man.

The Apostle Thomas is a good New Testament example of what God can do with a Spirit-filled Melancholy temperament. He is known as the doubting disciple because of his famous statement, "Except I shall see in his hands the print of the nails, and put my finger into the print of the nails, and thrust my hand into his side, I will not believe." (John 20:25) That is blatant unbelief induced by Thomas' doubts. Blatant because the words were spoken in spite of the Lord's oft-repeated promise to rise again and the ten disciples' assurance that "we have seen the Lord."

Actually, that isn't the only sample of Thomas' Melancholy pessimism. In John 11:16 Jesus insisted, in spite of his disciples' warning not to go "through Jewry" because they would kill him, that they should go to the home of Lazarus in Bethany. Seeing his Lord's determination and expressing his pessimism, Thomas said to his fellow disciples, "Let us also go, that we may die with him."

Humanly, such a man was doomed to failure, but such was not the case with Thomas. After being filled with the Holy Spirit, Thomas went out to serve the Lord faithfully. The Bible doesn't give Thomas' whole story, confining itself to the acts of Peter and Paul and their immediate associates. When I was in Madras, India, I saw the tomb of Apostle Thomas. The story of his ministry is regarded as authentic by many scholars.

It seems that after the day of Pentecost, Thomas was led of the Spirit to India where he braved all kinds of dangers and preached Christ in power. Many were converted and churches were established. Eventually, Thomas was martyred for his faith, and he died with the courage only the Holy Spirit can supply. The church in South India today is not the result of missionary labors, but dates back to the first century when doubting, Melancholy Thomas became a faithful servant of Jesus Christ through the filling of the Holy Spirit.

The Spirit-Filled Phlegmatic

The least apparent change of temperament when filled with the Holy Spirit will be Mr. Phlegmatic. The reason is that by nature he is calm, easy-going, peaceful, joyful and consistent—basically the qualities you expect in a Christian. Actually, unsaved Phlegmatics often act more like Christians than many Christians do. What then does the Holy Spirit do for the Phlegmatic?

For one thing, he will produce internally the calm, easy-going person that he appears to be on the outside. He will also overcome the weaknesses of reticence, stubbornness, fear, indifference and lack of motivation. Mr. Phlegmatic has the capability of being a very good leader; the Holy Spirit will enable him to achieve that potential.

The first fruit of the Spirit will go a long way toward motivating Mr. Phlegmatic. As his heart is genuinely filled with love for others he will be drawn out of his shell of self-protection and give himself more vigorously in the service of Christ. As his love for the Lord grows he will forget himself and take on, for the Lord's sake, things he previously rejected. With the Lord's power at his disposal, he will soon

LOVE

become a willing leader and a participant instead of a spectator. This gift of love from the Holy Spirit will take the biting edge out of his humor and he will become a source of pleasure for those associated with him. God will use him as a cheering, calming and encouraging influence on others.

The gift of faith provided to the Spirit-filled Phlegmatic will dispel one of his life-long problems—fear. Most Phlegmatics are unusually timid and afraid. Fear is a cruel taskmaster, and as the Spirit brings confidence and faith the Phlegmatic begins to lose many of his natural and learned inhibitions. Many a Phlegmatic has said, "I could never say anything in public," but when the Holy Spirit fills his life he finds speaking increasingly easier.

FAITH

The change doesn't come overnight, but gradually his concern for others and his desire to share his faith overcomes his fears. When he does speak he usually does an excellent job because he is well prepared and has his thoughts well organized. He will never be an extrovert, but he has a calm message so filled with facts and logic that it is well received by some of those missed by the loquacious extroverts.

GOODNESS

As the Holy Spirit fills his life, the Phlegmatic gradually comes to the full realization that he "can do all things through Christ who strengtheneth." This concept propels him through open doors of service, and since he is dependable and efficient even greater opportunities confront him.

The goodness and meekness of the Holy Spirit work together on Mr. Phlegmatic, causing him to think of others instead of himself, and their needs become a source of motivation. Unselfishness multiplies and his selfishness is replaced by a growing generosity.

MEEKNESS

Most people need self-control, and that is provided by the Holy Spirit. When he fills Mr. Phlegmatic's life he inspires him to finish the job and involve himself in many forms of service

139

previously omitted from his life. Many a productive and faithful Christian worker is a Spirit-filled Phlegmatic.

A good Bible illustration of the work of the Holy Spirit in the life of a Phlegmatic is easy-going, good-natured Abraham. This great patriarch was dominated most of his life by fear. In fact, twice in his life he was so selfishly fearful that he denied

SELF-CONTROL

his wife and tried to palm her off as his sister. She was such a beautiful woman that he thought Pharoah and later Abimelech would kill him to marry her. This cowardly man was later transformed so much by the gift of faith it was said of him: "Abraham believed God, and it was accounted to him for righteousness." (Gal. 3:6)

Actually, the Holy Spirit has some strength for every one of man's weaknesses. God does not want us to be dominated by our weaknesses and shortcomings. That is one reason he has sent his Holy Spirit. Most people tend to wish they had some other temperament when they recognize their weaknesses. It really doesn't matter what temperament you are—God can change you and make your life usable for himself.

This can only be done by the power of the Holy Spirit in your life. The most important single thing in your Christian life is to be filled with the Holy Spirit. Go back and read chapter seven again on "How to be Filled With the Holy Spirit," and practice his filling daily.

The story is told of a young man who asked an old saint he greatly admired how long it had been since he had lived a defeated day. The old man replied, "Over 30 years." He then explained to his young friend that 30 years earlier he made a vow that he would never let an hour go by between his sin and his prayer of confession.

If you make it a point to follow that procedure with the sincere request to be filled with the Holy Spirit (Luke 11:13), you will enjoy the victory and power of the Spirit-filled life. It will take time to become consistent, but remember, you have years of habit behind you that need to be overcome. You probably won't even notice the change when it comes, but some day it will dawn on you that in daily life you are a new creature, that truly:

> "The Lord hath done great things for us;
> whereof we are glad." (Psalm 126:3)